If This Is the

"LAST DAYS,"

How Then Shall We Live?

If This Is the

"LAST DAYS,"

How Then Shall We Live?

Jim Bard

To order additional copies of this book, contact:
Xlibris Corporation
1-888-795-4274
www.Xlibris.com
Orders@Xlibris.com
80585

Thank You

Heavenly Father who designed a wonderful outcome
for us who love him.

Jesus: friend, constant companion, and guide,
Who, above all else, gives me mercy, love, and hope.

Holy Spirit who encourages me when I fall
and restores me to a loving relationship

Loving wife Deborah who believes in me
And has disciplined herself to our life of serving Christ

Daughter Annette, who looked beyond my faults and has loved me
and helped me understand myself and others better.

Family, friends, and church,
You are an ever-present strength to me.

I am humbled and grateful for each of you.

CONTENTS

INTRODUCTION

I was born during the Second World War. I don't remember anything about that time. I was just too young. But I was raised during the Cold War era of the 1940s, 1950s, and 1960s. I honestly can't recall ever hearing the word *Cold War* being spoken during that time. What I do remember is the tension, the fear, and the anxiety—the anxiety that I felt around me from the adult world that came from that era.

I remember many conversations, news reports, and radio messages that address such issues as nuclear bombs, bomb shelters curse and what to do in case of an attack from Russia. In school there are many discussions around threats from other countries and philosophies such as communism that threaten our democracy, my personal safety, and peace of the world.

Don't get me wrong, the 1950s era had a lot of wonderful things that we've lost today, such as trout running in streams that were not planted fish and feeling safe at home without locking the doors when we leave home. Terrorism was relegated to the haunted house on Halloween. Christian values were practiced by everyone, whether they really believed in Christ and loved him or not.

I grew up in church. We were charismatic. We studied the Bible in Sunday school, and the preacher shared sermons on the Bible, and the Bible was explained and read at home by my father. The theme seemed to be quite often about the last days and how Jesus was coming back anytime. This, combined with the fear of being at war and destroyed by nuclear bombs, left me feeling very insecure and unsure of my life lasting even to the next day.

I recall receiving five dollars for having worked for my uncle one summer. I was fourteen years old. We attended church that Sunday, and the guest speaker was a colonel in the air force. He spoke about the Korean War and nuclear arms and the threat of global holocaust. He also spoke of Jesus coming back in the clouds, any day. As we drove home, I searched the clouds, looking for Jesus, and looked at my coins, the five silver dollars I received from my uncle. I could only think how I wanted to spend that money and enjoy it before Jesus came back or the communist started bombing us, and I wouldn't have the opportunity.

The common phrase used over and over was *we are in the last days*. I have always been told, and to this day I hear it often said, we are in the last days. It leaves me with this question: when are the last days? How do I know what the last days look like? What are the last days?

After searching for the answers, I have finally concluded that *we are in the last days*: even as I write these words, and you read these words. The last days, as referred to in the Bible, cover a period of time. That period of time is coming to a close. I cannot fathom it being another thousand years, nor one hundred years, and maybe not even another twenty years. I wish to share with you in the chapters to come. The evidence that will cause you to believe as I, that the return of Jesus in the clouds to gather us home is rapidly approaching. This book is about the signs of the time we now live in. The current events in the last ten years shed new light on the interpretation of the Scripture. The political, economic, religious, social, and other changes occurring right now shed new light on the interpretation of the Scripture. We can no longer rest on concepts developed over the last two millennium concerning the interpretation of the Scripture.

Josh McDowell has written a book called *Evidence That Demands a Verdict*. This great book has spurred a great deal of interest in the idea that the evidence of Jesus tells us to believe upon him. I think for the most part people search for evidence and then base conclusions upon that evidence. This seems to be the real scientific way to prove something. While I totally agree with this concept, in this book, I have chosen to reverse the order.

I am going to present the hypothesis, or the conclusion that I have come to, and then share with you my reasoning and evidence for believing that hypothesis. I only call it a hypothesis for the readers' benefit as I believe I have proven to myself those things that I'm going to share with you. Let me share some of the concepts.

I have come to understand that Jesus is coming back for a people who are pure and holy and have white robes without spot or blemish. There are no allowances for those who are alive and remain when he comes to be anything less. He has called us to be perfect and without sin.

The purpose of the last days is for that bride to grow up to the equal maturity of Christ. We may not feel that we are there now, but rest assured that when he comes, we will either be ready or be left behind. Jesus is coming soon, and we are in the last days.

I believe God the Father wants to be our God and for us to be his people forever.

I believe that Jesus is literally going to return to this earth and take his bride home to be with him forever.

I believe Jesus is referred to as the bridegroom, and we will have a relationship with him are part of what we call the bride. Someday there will be a great wedding feast to celebrate the marriage of the bride and the bridegroom.

I believe the beginning of the bride started with Adam and Eve and will be completed upon Jesus's return. Jesus returns, and the circumstances preceding that event can be seen and understood prior to his coming. The short time just before Jesus comes is well described in the Bible. There are specific signs of that time. We live in that time now.

I believe the Bible is the inspired word of God. I use word and not words because it is a single message from God about him, his Son, and the Son's bride. The Bible is not the Rock, but rather, Jesus is the Rock.

There are three keys to understanding all scripture.

1. In the beginning there was only God the Father, God the Holy Spirit, and God the Son.
2. God created humans so that someday he will be our God, and we will be his people forever in heaven and will never do anything to end that relationship.
3. Jesus ascended to heaven and is going to return for his bride who is equal in stature to Christ.
4. The Bible is the true and not finished story of God the Father and his desire for a people who love him the same as he loves them; the perfect Son and the revelation of his character; the bride and how she grows into the same character of her groom, Jesus; the Holy Spirit and his work to enable the bride-to-be like the groom: the wedding of the perfect groom to the perfect bride, and how they live happily ever after as God and his people in heaven.

This book is about that story. I present the evidence from the Scripture, from life itself, from history, and from current events that have convinced me of the preceding paragraph. It has changed the way I think and the way I interpret the Scripture. It has called me to a life more dedicated to being like Jesus. I hope and pray that this book will challenge you to make it all about Jesus more than you ever have before.

PREFACE

We cannot do the same thing over and over again and expect a different outcome.

—Author unknown

Since that time of the Reformation and the mass production of an organized Bible placed in the hands of the common person, the methods of interpreting the Bible and anything related to it have been the same. Each new theologian coming up in the ranks revisited the Scripture that was already expounded upon by the previous theologian. They would use the same method but take it one step deeper or wider in understanding and interpretation.

The new outcome they anticipated was relegated to an improvement on the old thinking but not an original or different outcome. In order for us to change the way we believe in certain areas, we must change the methods used to arrive at the conclusions we get.

I was raised in a well-known denomination. I was trained in a well-known Bible college of that denomination. For years I accepted and taught from the bases of which I was trained and the beliefs ingrained in me through the church. When I sought God for a new revelation, I found it was always tempered with the current acceptable theology of my peers in that denomination.

This left me asking many questions to which the answers fell short and incomplete at best. I discovered many conflicts of interpretations between the Scriptures. There are no conflicts or contradictions within the Scriptures of the Bible. There are many conflicts in trying to make harmony from various methods of interpreting the Bible.

I challenge you to look at this book as a fresh and different look at how the Scripture is interpreted.

When I decided to sct my beliefs aside and ask the Holy Spirit to help me understand the Bible, I got a whole new revelation. This book is a different method with a different outcome.

Instead of denying the truth of a Scripture, I look deeper and ask how can that Scripture be true?

> *1 John 3:9 "Whosoever is born of God does not commit sin; for his seed remaineth in him: and he cannot sin, because he is born of God." All Biiblical quotes are from the King James Version.*

This Scripture has always been interpreted as "Yeah, but we all sin." Because of our guilt and humanity and the way scholars have dealt with this Scripture over the centuries, we buy into a disbelief of what this Scripture really is saying.

My question is how can this be? My resolve is Christians do not sin. I believe I have found that answer by seeing a different way of looking at the Scripture. There can be no more excuses in the last days for living with sin occurring in our lives.

This book, with a different approach, will challenge those who read it. That is my intent. It will ruffle the nest in your comfort zone. It can change your life and help you find the freedom you seek in the Lord. For those who cannot accept change and find themselves fighting to defend what they believe, this book may be of no help.

This book is intended for those who seek the Lord, love him, and want to be ready when he comes.

Some may think that I am starting a cult. I can only tell you the difference between sound reasoning and a cult: a cult tells you to believe that what they're saying is the truth. I say to you: read this book, take it to the Lord, and let him tell you the truth. He will lead you into all truth, not me. I am just sharing what the Lord has shown me and what I believe.

Finally, please understand that I am not trying to prove the Bible exists nor am I trying to prove some theory that I believe.

The unbeliever demands proof. Without faith it is impossible to please God. We must believe that God is a rewarder of them who love him. If we do, we need no further proof of his existence or the Bible's authenticity.

If a Christian becomes elated over some new scientific discovery that somehow is supposed to make them believe stronger in the authenticity of the Bible, it becomes a confession of doubt.

This book is not written to cause anyone to believe in Jesus or in the Bible. It is written that the life you live in Christ might be full of joy, dedicated to loving him, set free from sin, and that you are ready for him when he comes.

CHAPTER I

Born to Sin

Romans 3:23

*"For all have sinned, and come short
of the glory of God."*

I was born into a Christian home. My father was a Pentecostal minister who pastored several churches in his lifetime. Consequently, I had the Bible's morals drilled into my head as far back as my earliest memories. I knew all the dos and don'ts. The first memory I have of the morals follows.

Dad accepted the pastorate of a small congregation in the town of Merrill, Oregon. It was the first week of summer. School was out, and it was a good time to move a family. So Dad, the happy new pastor, arrived in a station wagon with his wife and six children. The church stood on a street corner. It was a grand old two-story building. A tall white spire stood above as if to beacon to the townsfolk that we were there. The church was divided right down the middle. On the left side as you entered the front was the sanctuary. On the right side was the door to the parsonage. My room was shared with two brothers. Go in the front door, straight up the stairs, and turn right into the boys' room.

When you enter the church, you could immediately turn right and walk through a door that connected the church and the parsonage. It was very convenient as we didn't have to go out in the weather to go to church. It turned out to be too convenient for me.

They had a tradition in the church that I loved and then hated. The first Sunday of the month was Missionary Sunday. On this Sunday, the Sunday school superintendent would bring out a glass bank that looked like a lighthouse. It was about twelve inches tall. She sat it on the altar in front of the podium and then would ask for everyone who had a birthday to come forward. The birthday people would then come to the front and meticulously drop a penny into the bank for each year of age. We would all count out loud as the coins would drop. After everyone finished giving an offering, we sang happy birthday. It was fun. Some of the older folks used quarters, dimes, and nickels. Ageing jokes were told and all laughed. I loved the fun we had together in that little church.

Fall came and I enrolled in Merrill Middle School. That is when the big sin and guilt lesson came. I made friends slowly at school and so was somewhat of a loner. I ate my lunch alone mostly and didn't hang out at school talking to others. One weekend I went downtown and walked through the stores, just getting familiar with the area. There was a Ben Franklin store. The windows in front were loaded with enticing things, so I went in for a peek. There were games, toy cars, toy guns like Roy Rogers wore, and roller skates that just clamped on the shoes. My eyes filled with awe, and my heart filled with thoughts of fun and adventure. I lingered from shelf to shelf. It was a boy's heaven.

But then I saw something beyond my greatest imaginations. Something I had never seen. There in front of me was the biggest candy counter I ever laid eyes on. It had huge bins of all my favorite kinds of candy. There was candy corn, jelly beans, candy peanuts, burnt peanuts, chicken bones, Valentine hearts, jaw breakers, lemon drops, licorice in many forms, and more. And the best thing was, they were just twenty-five cents a pound and a person could buy one-fourth pound if they wanted. I thought I had died and gone to candy heaven.

There was just one problem. I had no money. We were a poor family. I didn't get an allowance. What was I to do? So close yet so far. I hated it.

Well, the next Sunday morning I found the answer. Now I don't know if Satan can give us a good idea in church or if God can give us a bad idea at all. Can Satan give us a bad thought in church? Well, a genius plan popped into my mind, and where it came from I am not sure. There was all of that birthday money. They never emptied the bank until it was full. I had to think this through carefully.

On Monday morning, before the family got up, I snuck downstairs. At the bottom I turned right and went into the church sanctuary. Oh so quietly I tiptoed up onto the platform, sallied behind the podium, bent over, and looked inside. There it was! The glass lighthouse seemed to light up as though the *Star of the East* shone on it. Angels sang, and the realization that I was going to score candy that morning made my heart pound and my mouth water. All those coins half-filling the jar. Perfect, I thought. I won't be greedy. I will just take a nickel. No one will ever know. I turned the lighthouse upside down on its beacon and wiggled it and came a dime and a nickel. Wow, I scored. No, I thought, I must be good, and I slipped the dime back into the lighthouse. Putting the dime in the bank left me feeling that I had put more in than I took out. How generous I felt. Proud of my discipline, I put the nickel in my pocket and slipped back to my room to finish getting ready for school.

I left for school early that morning, and my puzzled mother queried, "Why the rush?"

"Just meeting other kids to talk," I said shuffling out the door, feet hardly touching the ground. I made a straight line to the Ben Franklin. They were open. Up to the candy counter I jaunted and landed right in front of the candy corn. I couldn't wait. The pleasant lady peered over those tall stuffed bins of angelic food, and before she could get a word out, I spit out my needs. "I want a nickel's worth of candy corn." She smiled, weighed out the right amount, placed it in a little bag, and exchanged with me for the nickel.

It was a marvelous day. I don't recall a whole lot of my life from that year but that day and many others like it are sweet memories in my log of life, if you know what I mean. I loved those days.

Now you may see where I am headed, but I didn't. All I knew was I had a good deal going on. The best days were when I could score a quarter. Have you ever been twelve and eaten a whole pound of jelly beans by noon? No. Well then, you can't imagine how blissful a life God and the saints of the church provided me. This went on for a few months.

What came next was a real shocking surprise. One Sunday after church when everyone had gone, my father called me into the church sanctuary. There sat my mother on the front bench. Her face looked sad and worried. I had not seen her like that. She was always so happy. In her lap sat the lighthouse, her gentle hands wrapped around the half-full bank of Jim Bard, alias Sunday school birthday bank. Dad took me by the arm and marched me directly in front of my mecca. Somehow from the stern approach he was taking and the funeral atmosphere I felt, I didn't think he just wanted a part of the take.

"Son," he said in a voice that told me that the firing squad were loading their rifles at the very moment. He continued, "Sister Quinby says that in spite of all the people putting money in the lighthouse, the money has not filled the bank, and it has been several months. Do you know anything about this?"

"No," I said. I am sure the word came out of my mouth right, but at that very moment Satan betrayed me. Instead of helping me with a convincing story, he let God show my very own father the truth.

"Son," he said again. This was not the Merry-Christmas-son sound in his voice. It was now more like hell-hath-no-fury voice. He continued, "Be sure your sins will find you out, and if you lie it makes everything worse. Did you steal money from this bank?" In the beginning I thought he may have been asking a question; but now, in shock and horror, I realized these were not questions but statements, and I was standing there naked as a jaybird, totally exposed. Satan had duped me. It wasn't God who gave me the idea after all. My joy and wonderful experience suddenly turned into a torture of being held over the pit of hell. I smelled the smoke and was sure I was about to be tossed in with no chance of repentance.

Suddenly I was a believer. I confessed my sins. I sought mercy. At first it did not help. Dad was furious. He mentioned things like being asked to leave the church because his kid was a thief and how a pastor is supposed to be in control of his children.

He then addressed my sin. How could I do such a thing? I put a shame on all the family. I stole money that was to go to hungry missionaries in Africa. I took money from the others in church. When he was done demolishing every ounce of my sense of decency in me, he calmed down.

Having confessed the sin, and after making sure I understood how guilty I was, he went to the sentencing. I would work at chores and be grounded for a while. He covered it up by putting his money in the bank. No one was to know so that he could maintain respect in the church.

Years went by and I still did my share (and some of your share too) of misdeeds. I was considered the naughtiest kid in the family. I carried a lot of guilt. Yet every time I did something wrong I heard in the depths of my heart that voice of my father saying, "Be sure your sins will find you out." It didn't stop me from doing things, but it did heap a ton of guilt on me. I also became aware that I sinned.

The sin cycle kind of went like this, see if this resonates at all in your own life. I would do a bad thing. In my mind I would hear the quote, "Be sure your sins will find you out." I knew God not only knew what I did but at some point he would also confront me with the sin. I also knew that Dad or others would discover the sin. Yet invariably, I would find myself in church and some evangelist would ask people who had sin in their lives to come to the altar and ask Jesus to forgive them and get saved. I was probably saved twenty or thirty times between the ages of eight and eighteen. I told you I was pretty bad.

Now even though I confessed and got saved and heard Jesus forgave me of my sins, I was never confronted with the reasons for the behavior that caused me to sin. You see, I was keenly aware of consequence and forgiveness but never understood that through Jesus there was help for the behavior. I was just helpless to fix my nature and so God put up with me, covered up my misdeeds because Jesus had paid the price, and I got off the hook.

CHAPTER 2

Free from Sin

John 8:36

*If the son therefore shall make you free,
you shall be free indeed.*

But when do my sins find me out? I could never answer that unless it was in heaven when God plays that great video of our life for all to see. Then all my deeds will be wood, hay stubble because of the sin in my life.

So the answer became apparent to me. I must work at being good so that I will have rewards in heaven. Yet in time I learned that this too was impossible for me. I did not have enough energy or ability to be good enough for God. At the end of the day I always wound up in the hole. I sinned more than I did good things. Everything I read in Christian literature seemed to be about sins that we commit and how we can never be free from sins. I get saved. I'm supposed to be freed from sin. I sin again. Somehow, I am supposed to understand that though I am a Christian I am a sinner, a sinner saved by grace but never free from the bondage of sinning.

I cannot tell you how many times I sat in church and sang songs about being set free from sin. I would listen to testimonies of revered people in the church and how they were set free from sin. Then I listened to the sermon on Romans 8. The preacher would tell us we are never really free and though saved we still sin. A deep sense of discouragement sat in as I realized it was hopeless. I could never really be free from the bondage of the things I do, which is called sin. I'm not talking about me as a child. I'm talking about when I was a licensed minister in a prominent organization pastoring a church.

It drove me crazy. I wound up on a beach in El Segundo, California, saying to the Lord that I couldn't go on like this anymore. I was a Christian yet my heart was crushed beneath the weight of sin. I had been through Bible college, pastored churches, been an evangelist and preached the gospel; yet I was lost and defeated.

I knew Jesus loved me.

I don't know if you are okay with the statement that we all sin after we become Christians, but for me that is a weight I could not bear.

There on the sand at the ocean's edge I knelt and I said, "God, I am starting over. Help me understand." His words were clear. "Read the Bible again, and I will show you the answer."

I had read the Bible through several times, but this time was to be different. This time it made sense. This time I found freedom from sin. When I was done I was no longer ridden with guilt. I was set free.

This is my story of how I was set free from the bondage of sin. In John 8:36 I found that Jesus had and did set me free. All those things that I do, that I would not do, and all those things that I do not do, that I should do, I discovered had nothing to do with sin. I am a man of many shortcomings, inabilities, quirks, idiosyncrasies, and prone to many mistakes. This is who I am with the many factors, such as heredity, environment, education, and the simple composite of my ability to reason, for starters. We may fall short of achieving any perfection in this body or in this mind. To say that those things are sin after I have been forgiven of my sins is in direct conflict with the Scripture and the confirmation of the Holy Spirit. 1 John 3:9

I have been set free from the bondage of sin and do not sin anymore. I do continue to be human and make my mistakes. This book is an explanation of how I came to this conclusion. If you have ever struggled with this very complicated issue, I challenge you to read this book, and if you have further desire to discuss the issue, contact me. Jesus loves you and he will not abide in you if sin is in you. 1 John 3:6.

If you have struggled with this issue, or have struggled with sin and long to be freed since you have been a Christian, you need to read this book. You can be set free, my friend. You can be.

CHAPTER 3

Evidence of the "Last Days"

Acts 2:16-18

*"This is that which was spoken by the prophet Joel;
it shall come to pass in the last days, saith God, I will
pour out my spirit upon all flesh: and your sons and your
daughters shall prophesy, and your young men shall see
visions, and your old men shall dream dreams: and on
my servants and on my handmaidens I will pour out in
those days of my spirit; and they shall prophesy."*

The Bible is full of discussion regarding the last days. All the way from the Old Testament prophecy that said, "In the last days the spirit would be poured out upon people, knowledge should be increased, and wickedness would abound." In the New TestamentJesus, Paul, Peter, and John, especially in Revelation, spoke in prophetic ways of events pertaining to the last days. Some Bible scholars have ascribed these prophecies to time periods all the way from AD 70 until the present time. An argument could be made that the Church Age, the time period from Jesus' death to his second coming, was the last days. Others believe the last days pertain to the time after Jesus returns.

From the time of my early childhood when I can start remembering conversations about the return of Jesus, I associated it with conversations about the last days. At the turn of the century in the early 1900s, the world was witnessing industrial revolution, world wars, and worldwide communication through print and radio. This facilitated a tremendous amount of new information, which was probably overwhelming to most people. Think about it: for five thousand seven hundred years people rode horses and had little literature and *no* electronic communication; then in the span of a lifetime people had to deal with an overload of written information, massive airplanes and ships, some of which dropped nuclear weapons.

Is it any wonder that there was a spiritual awakening and renewal in America, which sent missionaries around the world with news that Jesus was coming and that the end was near? I can remember seeing people walking on streets with sandwich board signs that said, "The end is near." Every time I turned around I heard a new threat or experienced a new invention or heard a sermon that reinforced just that belief, and things were changing so fast that I knew end had to be near.

By the time I entered my midlife, and having heard that the end is near so often, every time something occurred, it seemed like this was *the* sign, such as Israel becoming a nation again. Well, I just knew this must be about the end. I believed it so strongly and was so amazed, and even disappointed, that once again I was sucked into the black hole called the "end is near." It seems that always the association with bad things happening in the world and the words "this is the last days" became wearisome from overuse. I even became hardened to the concept and felt that Jesus would not return for perhaps hundreds of years more, and that we could go on status quo for centuries to come.

The futurization of how the world would be and how we could live in that world, though it be twisted through science fiction books and movies, reinforces the idea the last days may be a long, long way away. On the other hand, there are those who say global warming is so bad that were all going to be destroyed by the overheating of earth in the near future.

It drove me to ask God the question: what are the signs of the last days? Are they all the bad things or are there good things as well that tell us that Jesus is about to appear? As I look at all the evidence, both external and internal, I can only draw the conclusion that we do live truly in the last days.

I mentioned internal and external evidence. Let me clarify what I mean by this.

Internal evidence is the evidence projecting the last days that comes from the Bible and speaks of the good news and the good things that happened between Jesus and his people. We, who are his bride, developing a personal relationship with the Lord is the internal evidence. I will share this in intricate details in the succeeding chapters. The relationship between Christ and his bride, and how close they are to becoming married, is the internal evidence most prevalent today.

External evidence is that which pertains to the signs of the times that are outside the relationship. These signs may be neutral signs, such as watching tree leaves turn brown and weathering; or they may be terrible signs, such as the increased terrorism and intensity of hostilities from others toward Christians; or they maybe even good signs, such as Israel becoming a nation, and the Jews returning to their homeland.

What I have seen occur in the last ten years, in both the internal and external evidences, are very different and unique from the things that have occurred prior to that time. Is it any wonder that all the predictions and prophecies that people have made over the centuries, and especially in the last century about the end times, fell short of truth. We tend to speak from the knowledge we have, and as time goes by we learn more and change our opinions. So what's to say this is just another stage and I'll learn more later and then change my opinion?

John 1:1 says, "In the beginning was the Word and the Word was with God and the Word was God." Genesis 1:1 says, "In the beginning God created heaven and earth." Revelations 21:3 says, "I heard a great voice out of heaven saying, behold, the tabernacle of God is with men, and He will dwell with them, and they shall be His people, and God Himself shall be with them, and be their God." What we learn from this is that at one point there was only God. God made heaven and earth. And the final outcome of all things is that he will be our God, and we will be his people for eternity.

So apparently God was alone, desired companionship from another entity, which was equal to him in love that would last forever. The question is: how does God, who is alone, find eternally guaranteed love by a person who chooses God and loves him the same as God loves them?

We need look no farther than the Bible itself. From the beginning when there was nothing to the end, where there is just God and his people, we find a beautiful and completely detailed story of how he achieved that great fete. It is a love story of how God the Father creates a perfect bride for the Son. He sent the Holy Spirit to prepare the bride for that great wedding (Revelation 19:7-9) of the perfect bride and the perfect groom.

Starting with the basic premise that God created man so that he might have eternally guaranteed love by a free moral agent. And the question remains, "How does he do that?" Look through the eyes of God and see his purpose, then come with me in the following chapters and see all the internal and external evidence of how he accomplishes his goal.

We will look at how he forms the bride from two simple cells coming together to the final presentation of the bride in her gown at that great wedding in heaven. This is internal evidence because it pertains to people who are a part of the bride. Like any other love letters, only those who are in love understand and appreciate what is being said.

We will also look at the external evidence: that is how those people who are not part of the bride will behave toward the bride. We also will look at how God treats those who are not part of his bride as well as those who are part of the bride, in today's present time and in the near future and for eternity.

Come with me, take the heart of a bride about to enter the chapel for marriage to her perfect groom-to-be, and see a new revelation of the times we live in. It will change your life.

CHAPTER 4

The Root of All Credible Evidence

2 Timothy 3:16-17

"All Scripture is given by inspiration of God, and is profitable for doctrine, for reproof, for correction, for instruction into righteousness: that the man of God may be perfect, thoroughly furnished unto all good works."

It is said that God's ways are higher than our ways, his thoughts are higher than our thoughts; and I believe that to be just so. While we cannot begin to understand all about God, nor envision his greatness or likeness or even perceive a bit of his death, there are things that he reveals to us so that we might understand him better.

In 1 Corinthians 2:9-10 we read, "But as it is written, Eye have not seen, nor ear heard, neither have entered into the heart of man, the things which God hath prepared for them that love Him. But God hath revealed them unto us by his Spirit: for the Spirit searches all things, yea, and the deep things of God." This Scripture is often quoted and misused in explaining how much higher his ways are than our ways. But the Scripture clearly says that while we can't imagine it God does reveal it to us.

Much of what I have to share with you is simply my revelation pertaining to God and his love letter called the Bible.

One thing that we should note is that we read the Bible from Genesis to Revelations and attempt to find a common thread. Unlike us, God didn't have to read the Bible to give us the Bible. Instead, he started with his final desire. "I will be their God and they will be my people," at the end (Revelations) of the Bible, and worked his way back to the beginning. The question of how did he achieve a creation of people who choose, as free moral agents, to love him and that through their love for him he would know that forever and eternity they would never leave him.

Unlike us with our fallible minds and limited capacities who struggle to this day to try to even understand ourselves, God is the master psychologist. He understands the end product of his creation and can work his way backward to the very beginning so that the outcome is exactly as he anticipated. Only he, in his infinite wisdom and knowledge, can perform such a feat. It stretches our minds to even try to comprehend such a complex method.

Science is based on taking two chemicals mixing them and discovering an outcome that makes something new. It is a constant trial and error to see what will happen. A scientist might have a theory of how the outcome will be, but they still must perform the experiment to prove the theory.

God works the opposite way. God says if I want the end product of this I must create something to get it. He knows every step of a process: from the first words of creation to that glorious marriage supper in the sky of Christ and his bride. He took each step from that end goal, step-by-step backward, until he got to the beginning point. Then he began creating to achieve his goal. Once he put things in place by creation, it became not a matter of creating more but watching his creation grow.

We start then with the basic premise that God created man and all things so that he might have companionship by a free moral agent, who loves him as he loves them, with eternally guaranteed love.

Did you know that God created the universe from nothing by faith? He believed in what he did not see because he imagined it. He then created it by speaking it in to existence. That is why it is not by proof but by faith that we please God. He wants us to believe in him even though we cannot see him now (Hebrews 11:1-3).

CHAPTER 5

The Setup

Genesis 1:1

*"In the beginning God created
the heavens and the earth."*

As we said in the previous chapter, God wanted an eternally guaranteed love by a free moral agent. That means that the people or person who loves him must love him by choice. Now it might seem easy to choose God if you knew God in his fullness versus any alternative to him. I suppose that is what one would call a no-brainer. It really wouldn't be a fair choice. And how would God know that you loved him as he loves you if the odds were still stacked in his favor so that it became a no-brainer?

So it would only seem a reasonable bet that God would create man, Adam and Eve for example, and place them in a situation where the forces of influence toward God or against God were equal. In order for him to create that situation there must be God, an opponent, and a place for the team to exist where they can make choices. We'll talk more in the next chapter or two about Adam and Eve and their choices. For now let's look at how he creates an opponent.

How does God get an opponent who will war against God, cannot be redeemed, and God would know this creation would sin?

Let's start from the beginning. In the beginning there was just God: Father, Son, and Holy Spirit. In Genesis 1-2, we read of the creation of the universe and the earth. I guess one could say that before he could stage the stage war, he would have to establish a level playing field. So God created the universe: galaxies upon galaxies, suns, stars, moons, asteroids, and, yes, planets including the earth.

The next thing God had to do was to create his own opponent. While God would not create evil, and I do not believe he *can* even create evil, he had to create an opponent who would become evil. He must then create good beings that lived in the fullness of his presence and yet could make a choice to sin. This is where angels come from.

God creates angels. Angels live in the full presence of God. One of the angel was named Lucifer, Satan, and the Evil one.

In Isaiah 14 we read, *"How art thou fallen from heaven, oh Lucifer, son of the morning! How art thou cut down from the ground, which did weaken the nations! For thou hast said in mine heart, I will ascend into heaven, I will exalt my throne above the stars of God: I will sit also upon the mount of the congregation, in the sides of the north: I will ascend above the heights of the clouds I will be like the most high. Yet thou shalt be brought down to hell to the sides of the pit. They that see thee shall narrowly look upon thee and consider thee, saying, is this the man that made the earth to tremble that did shake kingdoms; that made the world as a wilderness and destroyed the cities thereof; that opened not the house of his prisoners?"*

Many things can be deduced from the single Scripture. Satan, called Lucifer, lived in the full presence of God, and said that he would be higher than God. In his attempt to be the same as God he obviously made the choice to do what he wanted rather than what God wanted. This is the first recorded and original sin. It was not what Satan did but that he turned from God to his own desire. You see, instead of loving God and choosing to serve God as God had created him to, he chose his way and wanted to have his kingdom.

You might say, "Well, so why didn't God forgive him? What if Satan repented and said he would not do that again? Would God, could God even if he wanted to forgive, have forgiven Satan?"

The answer must be resoundingly no.

Since Lucifer lived in the full presence and knowledge of God, there existed no faith on Satan's part. Perhaps you might say God can forgive Satan and if Satan sinned again God could just forgive him again? That seems logical except that we miss one point. Satan did not love God with eternally guaranteed love, and he did not love

God with love equal to God's. There also was no way provided for atonement. And finally, there is no record that Satan ever repented or even wanted to.

The biggest problem was that Satan could never offer God eternally guaranteed love. The question of when will Satan sin again or try something new against God would always be looming in the realm of heaven. And you see, God's love is unconditionally given for ever and ever to them who love him with a love that is unconditionally forever.

Now while God did not intend for Satan to rise up against him, he also knew that Satan would. In response to Satan's sin, God cast him to a place we know as the earth. There, God gave Satan a place to dwell and rule over. See 2 Corinthians 4:4. There God proclaims Satan to be the god of this world.

Satan becomes the god of this world; however, there are rules that are applied to his reign. Satan is still subject to God's power over him. Satan can only do what God allows. Satan cannot reveal himself or his angels any more than God reveals himself. Satan can do nothing to a person unless the person invites him to do so.

The reason it's so important that God and Satan reveal themselves to mankind equally is so that you and I will make choices based on faith. We are not then swayed or overpowered by one side or the other, creating an unfair decision. This is the cornerstone upon which God receives eternally guaranteed love. "Without faith it is impossible to please Him" (Hebrews 11:6). The reason that it's impossible to please God without faith is that through faith in him and choosing him and loving him on this earth, we demonstrate to him our *eternally* guaranteed love.

The stage is now set. God has an adversary. The adversary and his cohorts (Satan and his angel followers) live on a chaotic planet and are set to war against God. This war cannot take place because God has already defeated Satan, confined him to a specific area, and essentially left him and his minions to be alone.

Now God is ready to introduce Adam and Eve. Before he could create Adam and Eve, he had to create an environment for them. In Genesis 1-2 we read how God created the Garden of Eden. This is the first battleground between God and Satan for the souls of people.

So God created the heaven and the earth. He separated water and land. He created the light from darkness. He created vegetation and animals. And all was well and harmonious. In it he placed trees, one which we know as the tree of knowledge of good and evil. And then God created Adam and Eve, and he placed them in the middle of the garden. Then he told them not to eat of this particular tree, giving them the reason that if they did they would surely die.

It is apparent that God did not disclose his plan. He did not reveal himself nor his angels completely. Nor did he allow Satan or his angels to reveal all that Satan and his angels knew.

God set specific rules of engagement among God, Satan, and man. God walked and talked with Adam in the cool of the evening. Satan spoke to Eve in a form of a serpent hanging from a tree. God said do not eat of the tree, and Satan said go ahead you'll get smart from the fruit.

Here is the first test of good and evil. God is good. Satan is evil. Adam and Eve got to know both. Adam and Eve were not good or evil, they just were. They existed as God had created them. There was a great difference between them and Satan. Satan was evil, opposed God, and sought to war with God to destroy Adam and Eve. God sought to have a good relationship with Adam and Eve. Adam and Eve simply needed to live within the rules God had given them.

They had choices to make. Their choices were good choices or evil choices based on who they chose to obey and believe.

We today are not necessarily good people or evil people. We don't qualify as people who are good or evil. We are all simply people making good or evil choices. Good choices are to do what God has asked us to do and evil choices are doing what Satan beguiles us to do. God is good. Satan is evil. We make choices for good or evil. This is the battle for your soul. We do not fight the battle of good or evil. that is, the war between God and Satan. We simply make choices that lead us to one side or the other. This is important to understand because it is in making these choices that God knows our love is eternally guaranteed to him. All of our choices are based on one thing: *faith*. We will believe good or evil influence and in believing make a choice to follow that. It takes the same amount of faith to believe in God or Satan, good or evil.

CHAPTER 6

A Bride for Jesus, A People for God

Revelations 21:9

"And there came unto me one of the seven angels which had the seven vials full of the seven last plagues, and talked with me, saying, come hither, I will show you the bride, the Lamb's wife."

In the beginning when there was just God the Father, the Son, and Holy Spirit, they desired a being to love them as they love, so they devised the plan we have talked about. We're going to look in depth now at that plan. The first thing we must realize is God said, "I will be their God and they will be my people." That was the father speaking. The second thing to realize is that the father would have a bride for his son. But wait, you say, how could God have a son when there was only God? Where was the mother? That is a fair question.

Jesus did exist as part of the Godhead. Perhaps he was like a son or perhaps he was an equal part of the Godhead, but there are two Scriptures we must bear in mind when we think about a son existing before the beginning of creation. John 1:1-5 says, *"In the beginning was the Word, and the word was with God, and the Word was God the same was in the beginning with God. All things were made by Him; and without Him was not anything made that was made. In Him was life; and the life was the light of men and the light shines in darkness and the darkness comprehended it not."* The fourteenth verse says, *"And the Word was made flesh, and dwelt among us, and we beheld His glory, the glory as of the only begotten of the father, full of grace and truth."*

From this we learn that Jesus, the Word, became flesh; he existed in the beginning. Now look at Genesis 1:26, which says, *"And God said, let us make man in our image after our likeness: and let them have dominion over the fish in the sea and over the fowl of the air, and over the cattle and over all the earth, and over every creeping thing that creeps upon the earth."*

When God said, "Let us create man in our image," he was speaking plural yet singular. It was the three in one consulting equally as one. Guess what? There are three parts to a person. What three parts do you supposed they are talking about? It appears to be

God the Father, God the Son, God the Holy Ghost. Each contributed to man that same part they contributed to the Godhead. The Father contributed the soul of man. The Son contributed the body of man. The Holy Ghost contributed the spirit of man. You see when Jesus came to earth he wasn't created in our image; but rather Adam was created in God's image, and therefore so are we.

Still not convinced? When the three Hebrew children, Shadrach, Meshach, and Abednego, were cast into the fiery furnace, people looking on explained with alarm, "Look there is a fourth man like unto the son of God." Daniel recorded this at least five hundred thirty years before Jesus was born in Bethlehem. How did they know about Jesus the son of God?

Philippians 2:6-8 says of Jesus, *"Who being in the form of God thought it not robbery to be equal with God: but made Himself of no reputation, and took upon him the form of a servant, and was made in the likeness of men: and being found in fashion as a man he humbled himself and became obedient and death even the death of the cross."*

I believe somehow people recognized a fourth man's figure in that furnace and also recognized that figure had the countenance of God and could only be the son of God.

I share all this to share that God wanted a bride for his son from the beginning of time. This was the point of all creation. God the Father's plan was to give himself a people and his son a bride. You see before he says, "I will be their God and they will be my people," he talks about a marriage for his son. Revelations 19:7-9 says, *"Let us be glad and rejoice and give honor to Him for the marriage of the Lamb is come, and His wife hath made herself ready. And to her was granted that she should be arrayed in fine linen clean and white: for the fine linen is the righteousness of the saints. And he said to me, write, Blessed are they which are called the marriage supper of the Lamb. And he said to me, these things are true sayings of God."*

Who is this woman who is made ready to marry Jesus? She is arrayed in fine linen, which is clean and white. Furthermore, the fine linen is the righteousness of the saints. Plain and white in this sense represents the purity of the saint.

I once preached a sermon in church about how we are part of the bride of Christ, and that we would be married to Christ someday. After church, a sweet lady came up to me and said quite seriously, "I don't like the idea of us being a bride, I have a grown son, and I cannot picture him wearing a wedding dress." Well, just because we are a part of the bride of Christ, I think, the fine linen and the pretty white dress is the symbol of our righteousness, and this dear lady must've had quite the misinterpretation of the Scripture we just quoted.

I think the more serious question to be asked is, "Who is the bride, and how does she get to that marriage supper?" I think it would be simple, no, way too simple, to say it is all believers from Adam and Eve to the last person born on earth. I know some people think everybody is a part of that bride. That God would not reject anybody from eternal life. I have people that share with me often about their concepts of who gets to be a part of the bride. There are many, many, many opinions on this subject. The best authority is the Bible and our interpretations of it, very much so that I will not try to identify whether you or I are in the bride. Rather I will try to show you in the next few chapters some evidence and discoveries both in the Bible and in the world that should help you decide for yourself.

I believe everyone who is a part of the bride has been qualified, whether they live in 5000 BC or the time of Christ or today, by God, and according to the times they lived and the rules God placed upon them during that period.

In the next few chapters I will share with you a picture of the creation of the bride. It starts with symbolically an egg and sperm uniting to begin life of the bride. That egg and sperm would be Adam and Eve. Through over six thousand years from that date when Adam and Eve were created until the time when Christ comes back for his church, we can see the bride grow from a single cell to a full-grown, beautiful, mature, perfect bride of Christ. The many people, perhaps millions or billions, who have contributed to this bride are like cells of the body that grows into maturity. This is alluded to in 1 Corinthians 12 where Paul talks about being members of one body. I think we are like cells of the body that grow from one cell, taking time to raise up a person, keeps adding cells and multiplying as the body grows. Upon reaching maturity some cells die and new cells come into existence even though the body does not continue to grow in size.

Check this out: there are eight distinct time periods recorded in the Bible where God made a covenant with man. Each of these time periods started with a covenant and terminates with the completion of the covenant or a new covenant being given. Oddly enough in each of these time periods, God's relationship with man begins and ends with a picture of a person growing up from the year of uniting of an egg and a sperm to a bride at the altar being married.

While there are eight covenants in the Bible, some referred to as dispensations, there are also eight periods of growth, which I have identified in a person. The way we treat a person in each of the eight periods of growth in their life, birth to marriage, so God treats mankind from Adam and Eve until the marriage supper of the bride the same way. In the next few chapters we will go into greater detail with each of these time periods. Theologians call these time periods in the Scripture dispensations.

I grew up in the home of an Assembly of God minister. My father did not have a great list of educational achievements. He did not have degrees hanging on the wall. He did not teach in a Bible school or college. He did however stay awake until two in the morning, night after night, after having worked a long day as a mechanic, studying the word of God. He also pastored small churches. As a result I sat under his teaching quite a lot. Dad was one of the greater theologians I have ever known. He introduced me to the concept of seven dispensations. He pulled out charts that had been prepared by other churches, and it seemed that it was a widely accepted doctrine to believe in the seven dispensations. I think if you approach any pastor who has studied, they probably will agree with you that there are seven dispensations.

After attending Bible college and pastoring/evangelizing for a number of years, my studies and relationship with Jesus led me to a path to say there are eight dispensations. That eighth dispensation was the Last Days. Traditionally scholars include this as part of the Church Age. However, under the rules of dispensations, the last days would be one. It starts with covenants and ends with a conclusion to the covenants.

The last days includes tumultuous changes in the church, in the world, and in the rest of the people who are not Christians. We will explore all the changes in a later chapter.

CHAPTER 7

The Garden of the Perfect and the Imperfect

Genesis 2:16-17

"And the Lord God commanded the man, saying, of every tree of the garden thou mayest freely eat: but of the tree of the knowledge of good and evil, thou shalt not eat of it: for in the day that thou eatest thereof thou shalt surely die.

This is the story of how the heavenly father raises the perfect bride for his perfect son. The Bible, often referred to as God's love letters to his people. And while this is true, it is also the revelation of how he *prepares his people* to be the perfect bride for the perfect groom.

In the chapters to come we will look at how God treated his people as they grew much in the same way a parent would treat a growing child today. We can stand to learn some great techniques of child-raising from the simple steps of the way God raised the bride. We will look at the growth processes and steps and see how God handles them to help the bride grow into a healthy mature and perfect presentation to Jesus. We'll see some of the same conflicts as people go through in their growing up process, and how God helps them deal with their conflicts. We will even look at the conflicts the bride faces today, in today's real world, as she prepares for her wedding.

It all starts in the Garden of Eden. God creates Adam and Eve. They have perfect bodies, perfect lines, and their spirits are untainted. God walks with them in the evening. They are placed in a garden where all things are provided for them. It is a harmonious, peaceful, and perfect place. It was Eden in every sense of the word. God also placed Satan, who appears in the form of a serpent, and perhaps gained familiarity with Adam and Eve to the point that Eve was not shocked when the serpent spoke. Perhaps Satan even spent many years gaining their confidence by just being around and talking to them before he sprung his little trap of deception.

The garden was perfect. God talked to Adam and Eve in the evening. And possibly Satan talked to Adam and Eve at other times. God had told Adam and Eve not to eat of the tree of knowledge of good and evil or you will die, but all the other herbs and plants it was okay to eat the fruit thereof. So one day Eve encounters Satan. He tells Eve she can eat the fruit of that tree and she would not die; but rather her eyes would be opened, and she would be like God.

Eve is now put in a peculiar situation, more peculiar that she has ever faced. Who does she believe, God or Satan? She hears what they both say, but, they say the opposite things. She is now called upon to make a choice. Up to this point in time she's never faced anything like it. God told her not to eat of the tree and she didn't. Now something new is introduced to her thinking. She has to exercise faith. Until this time all she had to do was obey. She was never confronted with a choice.

You know the story, Eve ate the fruit, shared it with Adam along with the story from Satan, and they ended up exiled from the garden. They made a choice based on their faith in what Satan said instead of what God said. They made a bad choice and the consequences we are now aware of. Thus was the beginning and ending of the first dispensation.

It started with God's covenant to provide for them a perfect place as long as they did not eat of the tree of good and evil. It ended when the covenant was broken. We call this the Edenic dispensation.

This scenario, found in the first three chapters of Genesis, is a picture of another scenario. It is that of conception, birth, and infancy of a child. It is a child that will grow over the period of six thousand years into a mature bride fully prepared for the groom. It starts with God creating Adam and Eve. They were the sperm and the egg of the bride. While they were mature adults there was male and female, one of each. They lived in the garden and grew in maturity and familiarity with their environment.

Adam and Eve were created in God's image. They were created with sensitivity to God, each other, their environment, and, yes, even

Satan. They were personally constructed by God, and God spent time with them in the evening. They talked and walked together, discussing perhaps the things of the garden and questions that might have arisen during the day. They, like a fetus in a well-protected environment, knew no threat. Just as the fetus grows and learns about the outside environment and begins early development patterns, so Adam and Eve lived in a protected environment in the garden. God provided all things needed for their growth: food, water, nutrients, and security.

When a baby is born that baby continues to live in a totally dependent environment. They depend on the parent to supply their food, water, warmth, and security. When they are uncomfortable they cry, and the parent is there to attend to their needs. Like a good parent God looked after Adam and Eve. While they tended the garden, they did not work the garden. They did not till the soil or work by the sweat of their brow, there was no pain and they did not age.

One day, however, Satan, having gained confidence from Adam and Eve, approached Eve with the idea of eating fruit from the tree of knowledge of good and evil. We know the rest of the story. Adam and Eve make their decision to trust Satan. Do you think that God was affected by their behavior? I do. You see, God was the parent who gave birth and life to them. They were his babies. He refers to all people as his children. Adam and Eve were the first born. God being the perfect parent as well as all-knowing God understood Adam and Eve's bad choice, lacking faith in God, and though I believe God understood, it was not his desire that they should exclude him in any decision that was so critical to their lives.

If it were not important, God would have said, "Oh, well," and all would have continued on as if nothing had happened. But something did happen. Adam and Eve disobeyed God's simple rule. The rule was the behavior motivated by lack of faith in God's words. Hebrews 11:6 says, *"Without faith it is impossible to please Him."* Faith is the essential element in every relationship. Faith in what God says, who he is, what he does, and what he wants, must exist in our heart in order to have a right relationship with God. We show him our faith through our love and devotion and actions toward him.

As a side note, all relationships are good when there is faith in each other. A husband and a wife cannot have a solid relationship without the trust that comes from having faith in each other. It's that kind of faith in each other that puts the other person first, seeks out their good, and connects them to make them one. From the time Adam and Eve turned from God in their faith and sought another, Satan, above him. They never regain the same trusting relationship they had in the garden.

Mankind from that day since struggles with lack of faith in the marriage. While it is the cornerstone of marriage, it has become the stumbling block of today's marriages. Is it any wonder that the world today has so little regard of marriage? I recently talked with a woman who believed that marriage should not last more than four years. I often hear when counseling couples before marriage that they are not concerned if it works forever because it's easy to get a divorce. The commitment to another based on faith in them is rarely seen these days. You know that kind of faith that says "I will be with you forever and trust you till death do us part" and then follow through with that.

Do you think that God was so nonchalant in his relationship with Adam and Eve that he could not be affected when their faith lapsed and believed a snake in the grass? Would we marry someone today with the idea that we will have faith in them only until a smooth-talking salesperson comes along with it slicker deal? Well, we are human. We suffer from Adam and Eve's sin in the garden, and we make bad choices because of it. But my friend, we don't have to. We can rise up and say I commit myself to you and will believe in you until death do us part. We can follow through with our commitment.

So the covenant of the first dispensation began with God saying do not eat of the tree of good and evil or you shall surely die. It ended with that covenant being broken by Eve, who ate the fruit of that tree. Adam and Eve could have lived forever in their perfect bodies, in their perfect environment, in total safety, and in a perfect relationship with God. From the day he first sinned by eating the fruit, the process of death began. It took a long time: Adam lived for nine hundred thirty years. We are not told how long Eve lived. You may feel that's a great price to pay for the simple act of eating an apple. But that's not the worst consequence. They toiled to work by the sweat of their brow and had pain and suffering in the bearing of children. Hey, that's not the worst consequence. They could never again experience that perfect relationship between them and God and each other again.

If you want a great relationship, try restoring your faith in your spouse and your God. Restore your faith in their judgment and their love for you, in their intent for your goodwill, and their ability to achieve and in their ability to have faith in you.

CHAPTER 8

Consequence and Fulfillment

Genesis 3:14-15

"The Lord God said unto the serpent, because thou hast done this, thou art cursed above all cattle, and above every beast of the field; upon thy belly shalt thou go, and dust shalt thou eat all the days of thy life: and I will put them enmity between thee and the woman, and between thy seed and her seed; it shall bruise thy head, and thou shalt bruise His heel."

When Adam and Eve broke God's covenant they changed the rules of relationship between him and them. God chose to do two things. The first thing God chose and set out to do was to heal the relationship between man and himself. The second thing God chose to do was eventually to restore the relationship to what it was in the Garden of Eden. This is because of God's ultimate plan for us to be his people and him to be our God and live with eternally guaranteed love—the relationship would have to be restored to the perfection of the garden relationship.

In Genesis 3 we read of the expulsion from the garden and the changes that occurred. The old covenant broken and fulfilled is now replaced by a new one. The new covenant addresses man's and God's relationship, the change in Satan, and the changes of man's relationship with each other and with the earth.

It's important to note that the old covenant, the first government that God made with Adam and Eve was broken but it was also fulfilled. They lived for a period of time abiding by the first covenant. They did not eat of the tree of knowledge of good and evil, they walked with God in the evening, and did not listen to what Satan had to say. Over a period of time day after day year after year, things became common to them. Perhaps Satan used the serpent and talked to Eve often, setting her up to trust him. Perhaps Adam and Eve then became vulnerable to something new being introduced. It seems plausible that they grew intellectually and with knowledge to the point that as Eve passes by the tree, Satan takes advantage of her vulnerability. He introduces a new thought and she responds. You see, he does that in all of the people throughout time and in people today as well.

I grew up in the Pentecostal movement at a time when long hair was considered a woman's glory and short hair was considered a sign of worldliness. All the women in our church wore long hair because the pressure of the belief, the ministers, and the men was so strong that the women agreed and wore long hair. I'm sure even the women who did this felt that was appropriate before God in their hearts. I did think as a young man it was odd that the women would wear long hair, but they wore it tucked above their neck in the summer because it was so hot. Before too long most of the women in the world was to wear short hair or hair in a beehive, and it became a strong issue in the church.

I was befuddled by the controversy. I began to question many of my beliefs regarding the way women and men with formed belief about their clothing and hair. Dresses were to be below the knees, short sleeves were taboo, jewelry and makeup had to be very limited, and certainly we could not go to a movie. All these kinds of thoughts had a common thread. We regulated anything that we did not understand or could not control. I think all these issues, and many more like it, focused around fear. There always seemed to be the fear that women's dress and behavior would lead to illicit sexual relationships and destroy marriages.

In time, after having gone to Bible college and pastoring for a number of years, I discovered that I had grown up. Those threats that I perceived from my training through childhood and the church were no longer threats to me personally. It seems so odd that the church felt short hair on a woman was beguiling and sinful and long hair a scriptural covering. But for me personally I found long hair far more attractive than shorthair. So I discovered what I believe to be a truth. It is not so much whether hair is long or short; it is how a person perceives it to affect them when they see it. So it is not the hair that beguiles me, but my sexuality, which I fear may get out of control. So I regulated the women around me to protect me from straying from my commitment.

What really happened here? I started out with a covenant, which my church prescribed to me. I adopted this as a commandment from God. I believed it and I practiced it. However, as time went by and I began to think more about all of the issues surrounding the way women look and my responses to them, I grew in understanding of myself. In time I outgrew my need for the covenant. By understanding myself and controlling my emotions I discovered no need to control others. In other words this covenant was fulfilled in me.

One way of looking at fulfilled is to say "fill full." When we are filled full with our experience and understanding of anything that we believed—and now no longer need that governing force—we are fulfilled. When we are filled full we become freed to move on to the next growth level.

As we look at the process of mankind maturing from that little babylike thinking into completed mature adults ready for marriage, we will see it's just a matter of going through the process of growing up. We learn a set of rules or disciplines that we must live by, and over time fulfill that process with full understanding and are ready to move on to the next level. Just as an individual grows and matures, so has mankind from the beginning until the day when Jesus comes back to earth.

God is such a good God. When he came into the garden after Adam and Eve had eaten of the tree, he already knew what had taken place, he calls for them. He arrives at his usual time, he does not show anger, and when they do not appear at the usual place he patiently calls. Adam and Eve finally answer and say, "Here we are Lord; we hid because we were naked."

Calmly God asks, "Who told you that you were naked?"

Through the course of the conversation Adam confessed that they had eaten of the fruit of the tree.

The very next set of verses reveals God's wisdom. He doesn't rant and rave about what they did. He doesn't go on and on about how they should have done differently, or how evil it was that they ate of the fruit. He never gave them a lecture on breaking trust or having faith. He simply let them know the natural consequences of having come to the fulfillment of their innocent relationship and what would lie ahead.

I have shared my belief that God knew and knows everything that every person is going to do clear through to the end of time. He is the perfect father. He understood his children, he understood their growth, and he was prepared to deal with the choices they inevitably would make. I don't believe he was angered, surprised, or caught off guard.

God always has a plan for the next step in his children's lives. This just happened to be the first. We have talked about the fulfillment of the rules Adam and Eve lived by. Now let's look at a little bit at the consequences, or those things that were lost and changed, after their encounter with God.

The first consequence was that God banished them from the garden lest they eat of the Tree of Life and have eternal life. The dynamics in their life now have changed in the most extreme of ways. They did not have seasons in the garden. All things grew on a perpetual basis. There was a natural ecology with perfect harmony among fauna and flora. Because they were created and not born of a human they were in perfect form. Because they lived in the perfect environment they would have lived forever. But now expelled from the garden the natural consequence is death.

God the perfect parent understood the impact this would have on Adam and Eve. He shared with them, I believe, as any good father would share.

When our innocent little child arrives at that time—you know that very first time when they look at you and question your word—you see the look in her eye and you know they have just figured out they have the power to do something, and it is not what you told them. They become awake and aware of themselves and their power. Every one of us has come to that moment when our child challenges us to respond. We may be amused or we may be tickled pink or we may be horrified. We may all react to it in a different way. The one thing's for sure: your relationship with that child will never be the same. They will no longer be 100 percent under your control and at your mercy.

God had this moment with Adam and Eve. It is not recorded how he felt. We only know that he reacted in their best interest to guide them to the next step.

So Adam and Eve grew up. They passed their time of innocence: from their creation to the expulsion from the garden. Genesis 3:7 says, "And *the eyes of them both were opened and they knew they were naked and they sewed fig leaves together and made themselves aprons.*" Now they have passed from innocence to the understanding that they made a mistake, and they have committed sin. As with all broken rules there is a consequence. And in becoming fulfilled in their life of innocence they find the need for a new standard of living. They are now more aware of themselves and their behavior. God too is aware of their need for change and a new standard.

In Genesis 3:14-19 we read about the consequences to Adam and Eve for growing into their next level. Satan also suffers consequences. In this passage we also see the next covenant, or the new set of rules for behavior, and how it affects the relationship between God, Satan, Adam and Eve, and mankind.

The consequences to Adam were that the ground was cursed, and it produced weeds that needed to be removed. There would be seasons, which would cause him to have to plant, care for, and harvest food. He would eat the food he raised. It would be hard, and he would work by the sweat of his brow to accomplish having food.

God said to Eve she would bear children in sorrow and that her desire would be to her husband and he would rule over her.

Satan received a more devastating blow than Adam or Eve. Adam and Eve's punishment was sickness, hard work, and death on this earth: then they would be redeemed unto eternal life with God. Satan's punishment was further restricted connection with humans, and he would be someday banished to a lake of fire for eternity.

Satan once lived in the full presence of God, but because of his sin his end will be everlasting punishment. Adam and Eve, who lived in the limited presence of God and sinned, would someday be redeemed to his eternal presence. Satan had all knowledge of God, while Adam and Eve had limited knowledge of God. Satan *knew* Adam and Eve had faith. Satan could never have faith because he was created into the full presence of God.

John 3:16 says it so clearly, *"God so loved the people that He gave his only begotten Son, that whosoever believeth on Him shall not perish but, have everlasting life."* There it is, that word *believe.* Whoever believes? Satan did not. It takes faith to achieve eternal life once we have fallen from grace. Satan, Adam, and Eve all fell, but only Adam and Eve could give God eternally guaranteed love through their faith walk. And only Adam and Eve could go from faith in God to a full knowledge of him.

God then said to Satan that someday the head of Satan's seed would be bruised by the heel of the seed of Eve. We know that Jesus was the Seed of Eve, whose heel wounds the seed of Satan, but who is the seed of Satan? Can Satan have children? If so, what kind of children?

John 8:44 gives us a peek at this. Here Jesus tells the Pharisees that they are of their father the devil. We will look at this in depth in a later chapter. As we go along, it will become clearer as to who are the ones involved in the families of Eve and Satan and how they bruise each other.

I find it interesting that God treats this situation much like any good parent of a small baby, just old enough to discover that the word *no* means no, for safety's sake. He sets boundaries, makes rules, allows the child to continue to explore their world, and watches over their shoulder to protect and observe.

When my son was about a year old, we moved from rural Oregon to Wilmington, California. Wilmington is between San Pedro and Long Beach on the waterfront. It was in a rough neighborhood. We had little money and, consequently, found ourselves living in an apartment in an all-Mexican neighborhood during the middle of riots. We are Caucasians and felt quite afraid.

My son had a crib that was next to a window. The ground outside the window was about four feet down. One day due to the heat, we left the window open during his nap so that he could be cooler and sleep better. Since he had never attempted to get out of his crib, we felt very safe with the arrangement. Soon he was quiet and asleep, so we went to the front room and relaxed as well.

After about an hour we heard a knock on the front door. When I answered the door, there stood a sweet Mexican lady with our son hand in hand. She recognized him and stated that she found him down the block walking.

Needless to say we were horrified. While it was reassuring to know that we had misjudged our neighbor's integrity, we also quickly responded to the need for tighter security. Our young son had just gone from a helpless innocent baby to a runaway child. He did nothing wrong. He just set out to explore his world. Up to this point we had no reason to be concerned about his abilities to imitate Harry Houdini. But now the rules had to change. He had fulfilled his age of innocence and was now forever locked in on the quest for freedom and adventure.

The answer was clear but not easy. Consequences were initiated for breaching his safety. The window was secured so that he could not get through it. Locks were installed on doors that he could not reach. We watched over him a little closer. When he wanted to explore, we were right with him.

After the incident was over and we sat on the couch recovering from the horror movie we just lived, we commented on the fact that we had just lost something very special. We lost the joy of believing, knowing, and trusting that our son is always where he was thought to be. Our relationship had changed. Please understand, it was great watching him grow up and go through the stages of life that kids go through, but the passing of each phase ended with something lost and something new to experience. I love my son so much. He has been the most wonderful blessing to me. When the scary path was over, it became exciting to watch him grow.

My son fulfilled his infancy. He was ready to take the next step (no pun intended) in his young life. He became aware of his desire and ability and grew up a bit in one afternoon.

This is just the way Adam and Eve did. God's young infant bride for his son just exercised the rite of passage from infancy to toddler at the end of Eden. Our heavenly father loves us even more than I love my son. He not only refers to us as his children, whom he loves, but he also refers to us as his son's bride: or in other words, we are his children and *we* are also his child that he is raising as a bride for his son.

CHAPTER 9

Adamic Dispensation: The Toddlers' World

Genesis 3:19

"In the sweat of thy face shalt thou eat bread, till thou return unto the ground; for out of it wast thou taken: for dust thou art, and unto dust thou shalt return."

When God sent Adam and Eve out of the garden he made them clothes from animal skins. For the first time animals gave their life for the welfare of man. It seems quite reasonable to conclude from the third and fourth chapters of Genesis that God instituted shedding of the blood of animals for a propitiation of their sin. God said that if they ate of the tree of knowledge of good and evil they would die. They were given redemption by the seed of the woman. However, until that day was accomplished they would sacrifice the life of animals for a covering of sin.

It is not clear how often that occurred, but I imagine every time they needed hides for clothes they went through the ritual of sacrifice, remembering what happened in the garden and why they were not in the garden anymore.

So it was that Adam and Eve left the Garden of Eden. They were expelled outside the garden to live. They had children and grew crops and raised animals for food and clothing. They apparently did not go too far from Eden as the crops grew easily and plentifully. God also still talked to them.

In Genesis 4 we read that God talked with Cain. Cain was a soil farmer. He raised crops. When Cain brought his offering to the Lord from the fruit of his labor, God had to make it clear that the grain was not an appropriate offering. Sin required a blood sacrifice and death. God wanted them to remember that he was sending a redeemer who would die for them. This angered Cain. He then became irritated with his brother Abel. God said to talk to Abel about it. When Cain talked to Abel he became so angry that he killed Abel.

In the next scene we find Cain being confronted by God. God asks about Abel, and Cain says he does not know. Cain lies! This is something new! There is something very unique about Cain's lie.

Cain must have been so innocent that he thought God could not see or know what had happened.

I was friends with a couple years ago who at the time had a son nearly two years old. The little lad's mother had made a cake with chocolate frosting for dessert that evening. When we arrived for dinner we met in the dining room where on the center of the table sat the cake. The bright little guy was all excited and wanted to show off the great prize that mommy had made. He quickly crawled up on a chair, brown eyes like boulders and the corners of his open mouth widely turned up, pointed his tiny finger to the cake and said, "See."

He moved his wiggly torso closer to the middle of the table, intently holding his finger in the direction of his obvious passion. He looked up to us and then back at the cake a time or two as he slowly inched closer. Finally just barely out of reach of the cake, his mother said, "No, Justin, get down, we can have frosting after supper." On that note she picked him up, and we all retired to the living room for a few moments of conversation.

As we settled in to the comfy chairs, Mandy explained little Justin. As she was frosting the cake, he constantly wanted to get involved. She gave him one of the egg beaters to lick. He loved it and wanted more. Since then he had a fascination with the frosting and has relentlessly tried to get more.

As we, men, continued the conversation about guy stuff, the gals arose and went to the kitchen to prepare the dinner. We got involved with ourselves and failed to notice that little Justin had slipped away. A startled sounding, "Oh, Justin," coming from the kitchen sent both of us men scurrying to the sound.

There was Mandy looking down at Justin. Justin was looking at his mother. They were locked eye to eye, no smiles, and no one blinked. Justin had rich chocolate frosting all over his face and hands. While he seemed quite satisfied he had that look on his face as if to say, "Why isn't mother as happy for me as I am for myself?"

"Justin," she said in an even tone, their eyes still locked with a mother's death grip tractor beam stare, she said, "did you get into the chocolate frosting?"

With no hesitation and eye ball to eye ball, Justin gave a strong and unabashed reply, "No."

Carefully Mandy picked up the little culprit and carried him to the dining table where laid the violated chocolate cake. Well, mother, father, and son had to have a short intermission from the get-together, and I retired to the living room where I could laugh with amusement. As I left the dining room, I had yielded to temptation just as my, younger but determinedcolleague had and swiped my finger through the chocolate frosting. I understood the problem. One taste and I was addicted also. I, however, more learned and devious than my wee predecessor, was able to conceal my sin and not get caught.

Cain's act of murder was wrong. He surely had more than one conversation about morals with his parents. Lying, however, was another issue all together. It probably never occurred to Adam and Eve or anyone else to lie. Cain must have felt a deep sense of fear.

God confronted Cain by asking Cain what he had done.

Cain had no answer. He could only stare into the eyes of a god who knew Cain's secret.

So God sent Cain further away from Eden. He told Cain that the land would not yield food as readily as before. And worse yet, Cain would be a vagabond and a fugitive.

Cain must have had the same sense of innocence as Justin. They were Innocent in that they did not understand the ramifications of lying and yet guilty of a very important error. His life would never be the same.

But what about the lie? Satan told the first lie but Cain's lie was the first lie by a human.

Death was already a process that began when Adam and Eve were expelled from the garden. Why did things change so much over the lie? You and I already know that lies are a complete breakdown of trust and without trust there is no basis for relationship.

Poor little Justin. Can you imagine him coming out to face us? As with little children, when they are reprimanded, they shy away to the corners and watch to see if the other adults are going to accept them. His guilt lingered, and it was some time before he had that twinkle in his eye and spark in his behavior back.

When God sent Cain away, Cain's response was fear of retribution from others. Cain was a grown man, yet his behavior and responses were that of a small toddler. You see at that time people had not learned social and moral skills. They had not dealt with sin as we do today. They were not so sophisticated.

God understood all this. He treated Cain's lie in the same manner as we would treat the first lie of our little child. God first recognized that Cain was now a willful sinner. God left the door open for Cain's salvation, but he allowed Cain the consequences of his decision.

The consequence of Cain's behavior continues. Cain was sent out from the presence of God, he had a strained relationship with other people, and his family did not inherit the birthright that was due the eldest son.

We who live today are so fortunate to live in a time when Jesus's blood cleanses us from all unrighteousness. We have instant forgiveness when we make mistakes. All we have to do is to ask forgiveness, and the Lord grants it.

The change in the relationship between God and man after the fall and expulsion from the Garden of Eden was a very simple one compared to today. They only had to sacrifice an animal for the atonement of their sin. From the time of Eden until the time of Noah, mankind learned basic relationship skills both with God and each other. Cain's lineage became obscured over the two-thousand-year time span.

Seth was born after Abel was killed. Seth's lineage had Enoch in it. Enoch never died. It also had Noah. After two thousand years of mankind doing what they wanted to, they became so wicked that God decided to basically start over with just Noah and his family. And so the great flood destroyed every living person except Noah and his family. This ends the Adamic dispensation.

Over the two thousand years, from Adam to Noah, man grew in experiencing and exploring their new world and environment until they were completely fulfilled in every way that they could be under the Adamic covenant.

Like two-year-olds left without parental guidance and control, mankind took a path of doing whatever came to them. When this occurs the outcome will largely be a destructive path. It was now time for God to begin training and educating his people and how to live with him and each other.

If we can look at this whole event from Adam to Noah in the context of the bride, and think of this progress of mankind as the growth years of a person and see the interaction between parent and child, we can see how God treated them as a good parent would treat a toddler. As this child goes from the innocent state to understanding the words *no, defiance, making mistakes*, and *paying the consequence*, he or she learns about shame, guilt, and fear. Like a toddler, she grows, her brain develops, and she reaches that level of maturity, where she is thinking in a more sophisticated manner and needs a broader spectrum of rules to live by.

We can see how she went from innocence to learning right from wrong in the most basic elements of living. The relationship she had with her parents in the beginning was that of being at one with them. But by the end of this time, having chosen to be independent has breached something very special—that of being one with the parents.

As we will see in chapters to come, planted in the heart of this child is the desire to be one with God and how that comes to be. When God told Adam and Eve that he would send the Redeemer to purchase what they had lost, he was not only talking about life in the Garden of Eden but, even more importantly, he was also talking about the relationship between himself and them. The shedding of the animal's blood in sacrifices, and the putting on of their skins around their own bodies, was the ritual to remind them that the Redeemer would someday come. For this child bride-to-be, it was the fault and dream that someday she would be one with God. That would come in the symbolization of the bride marrying the groom (Jesus) and being made one with God. See Revelations 19.

CHAPTER 10

The Noahic Period: Kids Will Be Kids

Genesis 9:6

"Whosoever sheddeth man's blood, by man shall his blood be shed: for in the image of God made he man."

The Covenant

The Adamic covenant has been fulfilled, and now we come to Noahic covenant. Take just a moment to read Genesis 9:1-17 so that you will know what I'm talking about in the next few paragraphs.

God has flooded the earth, destroyed all living creatures, and has saved Noah, his family, and pairs of the animals. The flood covers the earth and then the waters abate and the ark lands on dry ground. Sixty-seven days later God tells Noah to leave the ark, Genesis 8:13-14.

Noah then leaves the ark, builds an altar, and offers animal sacrifices to God. Here in the presence of the huge ark, Noah and his children begin life again. They take the time to honor God. In a quiet place God talks to his children, while they are emotionally, spiritually, and intellectually prepared to hear what he has to say.

God does speak. He sets forth the new covenants for his people. They were:

1. Would not further curse the ground for man's sake
2. Be fruitful and multiply.
3. As long as the earth remains there will be seasons.
4. Animals will fear man.
5. Man will eat animals cooked but not raw.
6. Man will have dominion over the animals.
7. God would not destroy earth with floods ever again.
8. There would be a rainbow as a signet of the covenant.
9. Man would judge man for wrongdoings.

God basically sits down with Noah and spells out the changes that have taken place and the new rules they would live by. The ground would remain the same and man would never have to fear total annihilation from God as long as the earth remains. Man could eat different food including animals as long as it was cooked. There would be a natural distrust between man and animals. God placed a rainbow in the sky as a reminder that he would keep his word. And finally, instead of God judging man, he tells them to set up their courts.

Some of these covenants last from Noah's time until the end of time when this earth is destroyed. Others were modified in covenants to come, such as the eating of meats. The Mosaic Law restricted some meats, while in the New Testament we are told those meats are okay again.

The Change in Relationship

The changing of the rules that man should live by was fairly simple. Unlike our constitution today with complexities that fill reams and volumes of pages of fine print that regulates the very minutest behavior, their simple rules said if a person kills another they too should die. The change that doesn't seem so apparent and simple is the most important change. That is the relationship between man and God changed.

In the garden and after that, up to this time, for over two thousand years, people did what they wanted, and God did the disciplining. God sent Adam and Eve from the garden. God told Cain his sacrifice was not acceptable and sent him away. It was also God that saw the wickedness of man that caused the great flood.

But now God tells Noah that they will judge one another and impose sentence upon one another and not he himself. God is actually distancing himself from mankind. While he still talks to Noah and to Abraham, he places the responsibility for punishment and judgment upon one another. They would have to solve problems that they haven't even dreamed of yet and do it without God's intervention.

What a shock! The last thing on Noah's mind, probably, was doing something evil. After all they were the ones God just saved from the flood.

Noah had a great relationship with the animals. The lions and the bunnies and the elephants and the mice gladly marched into the ark and were at peace with each other. Since the beginning of time the animals were not only harmonious with each other but were also not afraid of mankind either. That is why they were able to go into the ark without sedation or other forceful means. I doubt that Noah even had to have rooms for them. The fox and the chicken could lie side by side, and the fox would never steal one egg from the hen.

Until this moment, animals willingly gave their life to man as a sacrifice for sin. Yet they never had any fear and were at peace with man. But now, all of a sudden and without provocation from Noah, the animals went from the ark and became afraid. All of a sudden changes must have had a dramatic emotional impact on Noah and his family. Yet as Noah aged and his children created a lineage, the people adjusted. They grew and learned to live with the changes.

Preparing the Bride

Like a child growing up, the bride has grown through the toddler stage. She has fulfilled herself in understanding the word *no* and parental authority and discipline. We can liken the next stage of growth to that of a small child perhaps age three through six.

God being the parent is now ready to help the bride grow in some new areas. And just as a child in this age group begins to learn some new things and experiences new relationships so to people from Noah to Abraham have some growth to experience.

The child of this age group is ready to learn some specific social skills and independence. Even as Noah is told that people who misbehave with antisocial behavior would be disciplined by their peers, so it is when a child is in this three to six age group that they begin interacting with other children at times and places separated from their parent. They may be going to day care or preschool where they must learn a new set of social skills.

So the child whom God is growing to be the bride learns to interact with other children with acceptable behaviors. They not only discover that others may not like their behavior but will also react to their misbehavior. They also discover they may not have mommy and daddy to run to, to settle issues. Consequently, they learn to get along and work things out between themselves.

Just as God said to Noah that when a person kills another the peers must judge and that person who killed will be killed. That social behavior lesson filters down and applies to all aspects of life. We can see the growth and fulfillment of this lesson by looking at the story of the Tower of Babel. A group of people collaborated and started building a tower to God. God was not pleased with this as he told them to inhabit the earth and multiply. Consequently, God confused their languages and then they did disburse around the earth.

The child of this age group begins to experience periods of time away from parent, whether it be in preschool or just having extended periods of play away from parental presence. So God gave more latitude and independent time to this child, the bride-to-be, so that she could grow and become more independent.

The typical behavior of a child in this age group begins to interact socially and learns to build a project with their peers. Usually, there is a disagreement of how that should go and the lessons of working together begin. Sometimes it takes an adult's intervention to keep the children on track and from killing each other. What a parallel in behavior and consequences is seen in this time period.

Another thing that tends to be common with this age group is that they begin to learn dietary behaviors. Their taste buds are now developing and they develop likes and dislikes in certain foods. This is where they learn to eat healthier and less sugar foods. God spoke to the dietary needs by telling the people of this time that they could eat meat. This is a change from their diet in the prior dispensation. So the child learns to eat differently and with guidance.

The significance of this time period is that the child begins to learn how to make independent decisions. This is extremely important in childhood development. How the child grows into adulthood, learning skill sets of making good decisions. This is often done through the experience of making a bad decision with undesirable consequences.

From the time of Noah to the time Abraham is born, mankind has lived approximately three hundred fifty years. In this time period, this child whom God is rearing to be his bride has experienced growing socially, eating skills, consequences connected with misbehavior, and independence from the presence of the parents.

By the time Abraham is born and became a man mankind has discovered and experienced all the growth and lessons of these experiences. They are ready for the next step. So the bride has matured like a child and is ready for the next step.

Isn't it amazing how God helps us in our personal life to grow from where we are into that next step? Sometimes we don't really want to grow up. We would prefer to keep things the way they are. Just like a child who attends day care or preschool, besides that first day in elementary school, they're not quite ready for that challenge. It takes coaxing, preparation, and sometimes even the parent has to just leave and let the child and the teacher work it out. Sometimes God calls us to grow by taking us out of our comfort zone and puts us in a different social group. Sometimes we rebel. We fail to fit in with our new group. And we have to learn how to worship, how to entertain our new group, or even learn new customs in order to fit in.

It's not easy when God says to us it's time for us to grow and make more decisions on our own. Every person who wishes to follow God and do his will faces a time when God gives us choices. He will give us direction. He will give us parameters that we must work within; but he doesn't give us his immediate guidance, moment by moment, holding our hand so that we won't be scared and will know exactly what to do. Sure we all want this, but it is in God's plan that at some point in our relationship with him he sets us loose to start making good independent choices.

We call this a life of faith. "*Without faith it is impossible to please God,*" Hebrews 11:6. As I shared in chapter 1, Adam and Eve acted in faith. They put more faith in what Satan said than what God said. There were extreme consequences. In every person's walk with the Lord, we must exercise independence, good decisions based on faith in Jesus and his word. The lesson that we must learn from this time in our maturing process is that as we grow we must take responsibility for our behavior, while at the same time knowing and believing that God, our heavenly father, will always be there to help us when we really need him. He gives us direction. He gives us guidance. He made sure that we are safe in him. He also helps us get all that we need to mature to the fullness of this stature of Christ.

It is so easy to say in our lives, "I like this level that I'm living at and I don't want to have to grow, leave my comfort zone, and face the challenges of change God calls me to." Yet how shall we receive the reward of the bride if we do not choose the path that leads to be the chosen one by the groom.

Would you just take a few minutes alone with the Lord now? If you've been struggling with questions about does God want you to do this thing or this other thing, perhaps it's a question of what is right or wrong for you to do. Perhaps you're unsure that God has called you to do something and you're struggling with that question, is this God or not?

I want to challenge you with this thought. These struggles are the same kind of struggles the little children go through when parents begin separating from them, and they experience their independence. They begin to question, "Is this what mommy wants or what daddy wants me to do?" They asked themselves, is this okay for me to do or will I get in trouble?

If you are at a crossroads of choice, and you ask the Lord to guide you, he will. If you've asked over and over and you still are unsure, consider that he has already given you guidance, and you are just afraid to act. It is important to make a good decision and make a choice that leads you closer to him. However, more important than the perfect choice you make is that you act in faith, believing.

Read Hebrews 11. This is about people who made choices. Not once in this chapter does God say he counted their choice as righteousness. He only says he counted their faith as righteousness. You see in every step of our life from the point where God begins to give us direction and choices until the day he calls us home, he wants us to make choices based on faith in him and for no other reason.

As you consider this, and the choice in front of you, fear not. He is with you. Do all that you do as unto the Lord in faith, believing. If you find that your choice led you to a dead end, and you realize that you must backtrack and go another direction, do not fear that you have sinned. Believe in the Lord.

Know this: God is not displeased but is, on the contrary, quite pleased because you acted in faith. This experience will help you grow and mature in him. Just like the people at the Tower of Babel; they made a bad decision, and God had to redirect them. However, God never destroyed them nor rejected them. He still recognized his people as part of the bride. Those very people are part of us today who are a part of the bride. Think of them spiritually as a phase in our spiritual childhood and we today are as mature adults. The bride made a mistake by erecting the Tower of Babel. But through it the bride grew and learned a lesson that applies to everything we do as the bride today. Our understanding and maturity as Christians can only be because those people had faith and acted. They learned a lesson and grew, and the next thing we see God calls Abraham and gives the bride a new challenge. Oh, how he loves us so much that so large a mistake that caused him to confuse the language of people did not stop him from helping the bride to grow.

He loves you today, as you read this book, every bit as much as any person from any time in history. Believe him, trust him, show him your love and trust by acting in faith.

CHAPTER 11

Abrahamic Covenant: Family and Home

Genesis 25:5

"And Abraham gave all that he had unto Isaac.

Covenant 1

The Abrahamic dispensation covered a time period of about five hundred to six hundred years. It started with Abraham's call from God to leave Ur and go to Canaan and ended with Moses leading the children of Israel out of Egypt. Important events to note for this time are: covenant with Abraham regarding his lineage, the birth of Ishmael and Isaac, the life of Jacob and Joseph, and the years of captivity in Egypt.

There is the sense of a new beginning for God's people with Abraham. God says that he will be the father of many nations and his seed will be as the stars of the heavens and the sand of the sea shore. They are without number. Some scholars say this is the beginning of an earthly lineage through Ishmael and a spiritual lineage through Isaac. I hope to present another picture in this chapter.

Many religions refer to Abraham as the father of their religion. It would almost seem that this is where we come to a common heritage in the religions. From Adam to Abraham it was a lineage handed down, where all people had a common family history. But Abraham had two sons (Ishmael and Isaac) who had two different mothers and developed two different characters in which we see two different families develop. One mother was a wife and the other mother was a servant.

When God dispersed the people at the Tower of Babel, there were many families. They went their way across the face of the earth. But of all of the families, only one family was chosen to carry the seed of the Redeemer: that was the family of Noah, Tarah, and Abraham. Now we see God's chosen one, Abraham, have two separate families of significance. Once again there is a chosen one.

In Genesis 16 God says to Hagar that she will have a son and through him her seed would be so great it could not be numbered. He also said that she would call his name Ishmael because the Lord understood her affliction. And finally God concluded that Ishmael would be a wild man, his hand would be against every man and every man's hand against him and he would dwell in the presence of all of his brothers.

In Genesis 17 Abraham thanks God for Ishmael believing this was God's promise. But God says not so and tells Abraham that he would bear a son with Sarah and his name would be Isaac and God would establish his covenant with him for an everlasting covenant and with his seed after him. Later after Abraham was willing to sacrifice Isaac, trusting God for a provision of the lamb, God told Abraham that his seed would be as the sand of the sea and the stars of the heavens.

I believe that God was referring to the different lineage's being both physical and spiritual. The physical families would both have great numbers as the sand of the sea, meaning earthly or physical. They would also be different spiritually and vie for the affections and preference of God.

Covenant 2

God promised Abraham land. For the next four hundred years Abraham and his descendants grew wealthy and had their land. Even after the captivity by the Egyptians, where they were in slavery, they left Egypt with great wealth. Read Genesis 13 and Exodus 11.

God gave Israel their space. He promised it to all generations to come in the line of Isaac and Jacob. The Israelites became a chosen people. Ishmael and his descendants have fought over that land even to this day. Other children of Abraham and their descendants along with other families fight for that land even today. It is like a sibling rivalry for the room they each want in a big house. God planned for each of them to have their space, but for some reason that sibling rivalry for the best room continues. It is so strong that the radical Muslim people have vowed to destroy all the Israelites.

Covenant 3

God institutes a practice called circumcision. Only Isaac was to be circumcised by Abraham. Ishmael was born first, and God did not give Ishmael the promise of burying the seed that produced Jesus. This was given to the seed of Isaac. But the covenant between Abraham and God that Isaac would be the chosen family was signified by circumcision. This practice is carried on even today to signify our relationship with God. Oddly enough the Muslims practice circumcision more than the Jews and far more than Christians today.

And the People Grew

A new covenant between God and man is a window through which we can peek to see what is going to happen to God's people. As we peer through the window of this covenant, we can see some very definite things people are going to go through.

They will learn how to take care of their land and to maintain their presence in it. Their main focus will be on their growth in the family. Their family growth will focus on two things: (a) building of a family by population growth and (b) building a family with moral values.

They will also learn about themselves. This time period is filled with sexual issues. It seems that God is dealing with mankind and the issues of preadolescent sexuality.

Abraham is instructed in the way of circumcision. He also gives his wife to be a wife to another man in order to live. Lot lives in a homosexual city. Lot also sleeps with his daughters. Jacob works hard to get a woman he loves but is duped into marrying another woman. Abraham wants a baby but is convinced to sleep with a servant instead of his wife. All could have disastrous effects, yet God is present and brings his people through it.

We also see another thing happening, which is very significant. Fighting among people for the birthright and the blessing is seen with Isaac and Ishmael, Esau and Jacob, and Joseph and his brothers. All this is done for the blessing of the lineage of the Redeemer.

From Adam to Abraham there was no fighting for the right of God's blessing. Everybody was blessed and unaware of what was ahead. With the introduction of the term God's chosen people, a rivalry starts. Some say this is the difference between Jews and gentiles. I think this concept of Jews versus gentiles is too small.

I prefer to think that everyone who played a part in the bride, from Adam to the last person born before Jesus returns to take the bride away, is a part of this great group known as the bride. It includes Adam, Noah, Abraham, Moses, Jesus, David, and all those who have given their hearts to the Lord. Jesus is the center of it all. We who are in the family need only to believe on Jesus as the Messiah/Savior to be a part of the bride.

Since Abraham some people want to claim the right to be God's chosen without believing on the Son of God, the Groom. We will address this more in another chapter.

Growing the Bride

So what is being a preteen all about? You know, self-discovery of emotions, getting our own room for privacy, siblings, fads, peer pressure, sexual awareness, hormonal development, making good choices, disconnecting and reconnecting from parents, and making our decisions based on little knowledge but a lot of feelings.

Abraham is given his land. This bride-child is given her room to enjoy, care for, seek solace in, enjoy privacy in, begin ownership of possessions, and make it a part of her life.

Jacob's children had problems in his possessing the land and lost it. They ended up losing the land and spending four hundred years bunked in with the Egyptians. Typical of a middle school-aged or junior high-aged child when they finally get a room to themselves. Their first experience in ownership and they had to learn the hard way.

This time zone is loaded with sexual relationship stories for the first time in Bible. Issues of awareness that come to the young preadolescent bride-to-be are male anatomy (circumcision), homosexuality (Sodom and Gomorrah), pregnancy awareness (Sarah and Hagar), sleeping around (Abraham gives Sarah to another man), dating and betrayal (Jacob with Rachel and Leah), and molestation and incest (Lot and his daughters).

The first war is recorded. It is one thing for kids to whine about their siblings to mommy and daddy, but now we are talking about swords, knives, and clubs in a battle that leaves many dead bodies. This occurred when Abraham had to rescue Lot. We also see armed kingdoms emerge. It is at this time in the hormone driven, emotionally charged time of the developing adolescent that peer rivalry, gang mentality, and extreme jealousy begins to develop that serious fighting gets introduced.

Finally there is the beginning of competition and vying for the boyfriend that starts at this age. Courtship begins now with the introduction of dating, fads, peer pressure, and all that goes into discovering the opposite sex and our sexuality

It is an interesting parallel with the introduction of Isaac and Ishmael. Isaac received the blessing of God and the promise was given a sign called circumcision.

Genesis 17:20-21 (KJV) "*And as for Ishmael, I have heard thee: Behold, I have blessed him, and will make fruitful, and will multiply him exceedingly; twelve princes shall he begat, and I will make him a great nation. But my covenant will I establish with Isaac, which Sarah shall bear unto thee at this set time in the next year.*"

Genesis 16:11-12 (KJV) shows God's position on Ishmael and his descendants. "*And the angel of the Lord said unto her (Hagar), Behold, thou art with child, and shall bear a son, and shall call his name Ishmael; because the Lord hath heard thy affliction. And he will be a wild man, his hand will be against every man, and every man's hand will be against him; and he shall dwell in the presence of all his brethren.*"

The descendants of Abraham people, who are not Jews, also lay claim to being God's chosen ones and call all others infidels. From that day until now and until the time Jesus comes for his bride, they will war against the Jews and all who align with them. Though they could recognize Jesus and become part of the bride they take their own way. It is a way of force to get their own way and capture God instead of loving him and accepting his will as stated in Genesis 16. They are part of who Jesus talked about in Matthew 11:12 (KJV) " . . . the Kingdom of God suffereth violence and the violent take it by force."

With Isaac we see the awareness of the bride as she starts the journey of becoming a woman. With Ishmael we see that there are others emerging who also want to have the same suitor and eventually, like women, will vie for same man to be their husband.

Something very significant happens here. God recognizes that Isaac's lineage will bear the Redeemer/groom (Jesus). Those who believe in Jesus as the Messiah and Savior become part of the bride. The groom will search the many religious groups who lay claim to God who are as hopeful to be his forever. However, in Revelation we read that he will be Father God only to those who are at the marriage supper with Jesus. And all those who are there are the bride. So only those who believe on Jesus are in the bride.

So this fight for the groom, between the true brides-to-be, that God is culturing and raising and the other religions and sects of the world, like preadolescents, are developing a rivalry. Isaac and Ishmael are the beginning of a long-standing rivalry with all the emotions, hormones, fickleness, and territorial positioning of preadolescents. Yet the lines have been drawn and the personalities are going to show up more and more as the bride matures and the rivals mature.

The people grew into a nation and accomplished all that they could with the covenants God gave them. They matured to the level that they were supposed to. Since they accomplished God's goals they were ready to move on to the next level. They were ready to graduate from junior high.

Reflection

Have you been faced with a situation where someone says to you that there are many ways to God, or that we are all brothers and sisters on this earth? Do you have a child or sibling that doesn't confess Jesus as their personal savior? Do these people seem set in their ways and unapproachable?

I am guessing it hurts you deeply as you agonize over their eternal destiny. You see them not making their way to heaven, and you weep for them as I have for those I love who reject Christ. Remember, those who reject the way of Christ are rejecting him.

Perhaps you have had arguments over this with them. Perhaps you have tried fear tactics, love tactics, fire and brimstone as well as prayer and scripture. Well, it is easy to resort to fighting over all this. That is what Ishmael wants. Look back. What are we doing?

The Ishmaelites are not our enemy. Satan is our enemy. "We wrestle not against flesh and blood, but against principalities and powers" (Ephesians 6:12). We love all people and want them to know Christ and be a part of the bride. We hate the evil one and all the evil that he causes people to perform. Keeping that focus helps us not enter in to the juvenile and petty fights over religion.

Even arguing doctrine among ourselves falls into this category. One Muslim, on television, in an interview said, "Christians can't even agree among themselves on their beliefs." It seems that if God is love and Jesus, his son, wants us to love one another then we, the bride, should pay attention to what the groom is wanting lest he turn to another.

CHAPTER 12

Mosaic Covenant: Adolescent Teen Years I

Exodus 24:12

"And the Lord said unto Moses, come up to Me into the mount, and be there: and I will give you tables of stone, and a law, and Commandments which I have written; that thou mayest teach them."

The Mosaic covenant begins with Moses leading the children of Israel out of Egypt and ends with the crucifixion and resurrection of Christ. It is also known as the law age. In a teenager's life, it covers roughly the ages of thirteen to nineteen years of age.

The Jewish people have graduated and fulfilled the requirements God had set for them in the last covenant. Now they are ready to enter high school. Moses comes on the scene and leads them out of one school and on to the next. He led the people from Egypt to Canaan, the land that God promised to Abraham and Isaac.

As we saw in the previous chapter there were a handful of covenants and five hundred years to fulfill them. The next phase takes nearly one thousand five hundred years and instead of a few covenants there are thousands. I cannot cover them all individually. I will give you an overview of those that pertain to the growth of the bride.

Covenants

It starts with the institution of the Passover, which will be observed every year as long as the Jews are on this earth. As soon as they are out of the country God gives them the Mosaic Law. These are covenants that cover all aspects of behavior: social, spiritual, legal, financial, family, and many others. It gets into detail of each aspect, far greater than anything before. Every aspect of a person's life was covered by some point of the Mosaic Law.

There were also consequences for breaking the law. Penalties included anything from sacrificing a bird to death. Some penalties for breaking the rules required restitution. Some laws governed family responsibilities. Some laws spelled out in detail how people dressed for certain occasions. What people ate was governed by rules. They were told what day they went to church and where to sit when they got there. There was not anything left to guess or self-interpretation.

The children of Israel were not unfamiliar with complaining. As soon as they came to the Red Sea they complained that they were going to drown. When Moses went to the mountain to receive the Ten Commandments, they whined that he was gone too long. When they came to Kadesh-Barnea, the spies complained that the people were too big to fight. In the desert they whined about no food, and after God gave them food they complained about it being boring.

Israel was commanded to honor their father and mother. Obedience was not enough. It also included treating them with respect and following their parent's values. Jealousy was addressed. They were not to covet anything someone else had.

I think we get the point. The how to behave manual was published, and God expected the Israelites from Moses until Jesus to abide by them. Read the books of Exodus, Leviticus, and Deuteronomy.

The Other Kids

The other kids, the people that are left in Canaan when Jacobs's family moved to Egypt, have taken over the land. These include the Ishmaelites, children of Abraham's concubines, and other people unrelated to Abraham, Isaac, or Jacob. They also built weapons and developed armies. When the Israelites return to Canaan they have a fight on their hands. Once again, the other brides-to-be are wanting what the chosen one possesses. The stakes are a little higher. Instead of wanting a blessing, they want the real estate. It is more sophisticated and expanded now than it was with Ishmael and Isaac. It is the turf war of many families.

The Educational Journey

When the Israelites finally start the process of living in their land and developing communities, alliances, and governments, they soon learn the reality of growing up. They have a tumultuous time gaining their land and keeping their land. Read Joshua and Judges. They had multiple episodes of making bad choices, doing the wrong thing, being taken captive, repentance, and deliverance.

No matter how often though, God, like a good parent, would always bring a hero of the day, such as Gideon or Sampson, and the Israelites would be set free and restored to their right standing.

The journey of the Jews was one of progress in growth in education in relationships with God and others. Each time they went through a cycle of learning they grew up a little more.

The Teen Bride-To-Be

This young lady who will someday be the bride of Christ is now entering her (so to speak) high school years. Let's compare the journeys of the Israelites to a teen's life. There are some startling similarities.

The behavior of the Israelites entering Canaan after leaving Egypt, as they face new experiences, challenges and difficulties, is somewhat erratic and driven by trial and error. Having little or no experience in dealing with the things they faced they had to learn as they go. So adolescents going into their teen years facing absolutely new trials, challenges, and experiences, with no experience to help guide them. They need a manual. Just as God gave Israel a manual so the adolescent teen is given a manual. It is called "Parents and What They Say Goes." While most parents give their teen child a certain amount of latitude and choice, their decisions are closely monitored and guided and modified as needed for their safety, protection, and opportunity to learn to fail and grow without harm or as little damage as possible.

This manual, or guide to life, is being written as they go. The lessons in this manual come from education by experience, classroom setting, input by parents, teachers, peers, and other people the adolescent listens to.

As an adolescent being raised by God, this heavenly father raises his child to be the best and perfect presentation for that groom who will someday come calling and court the bride-to-be. As we can see in the times of the settling of Israel, God trains his adolescent child by giving her principles to live by, giving her classroom education, and allowing experiences in failure and overcoming.

There is a cycle that we as adolescents go through that God's adolescent child went through. It starts with interests then becomes a task, which becomes an experience. The experience shapes behavior. The behavior may need modification. For out of behavior comes beliefs, which may be correct or maybe erroneous. Consequently, it may take many similar experiences to learn one lesson. That is called being an adolescent

I do not say all this with the pretense that I understand psychology. The observation is that what the Israelites went through in this particular time is very parallel to what teenagers go through. Can you see God working to grow his bride? That perfect bride, whom Jesus is coming for, does not happen overnight and does not just occur by happenstance. We the bride of Christ, from Adam until the last person born before Jesus comes to claim his bride, are a collection of the process of God raising a child into an adult that is groomed and prepared to be the perfect match and mate to his son Christ Jesus.

Another thing to note is that there are three players vying for the right to God and his son Jesus. The first is, of course, the future bride. We are the descendants of Abraham, and we claim that birthright with the Jews to God. The Jews along with Christians are part of the true bride-to-be.

The second are the descendants of Ishmael and other direct descendants of Abraham who claim the right to God through Abraham. The difference between Christians and the others is clearly seen in how they grow through adolescence into adulthood and prepare for marriage.

The third are those who would claim God yet do not recognize the God of Abraham, but rather choose to believe only in their concepts of God as they create him to be. These are people who are not of Abraham's descent.

When the children of Israel came back to Canaan, their enemies were the descendants of Ishmael that had settled in that area and others who had settled in that area who are not descendants of Abraham. It is important to understand that the last two groups are like suitors for God's son: all wanting to please God and have God's favor without coming through the preparation by God through Jesus.

In this time span of adolescence, the production of new hormones introduces the awareness of new feelings, emotions, and thoughts that prompt interactions between males and females. Drives to compete, perform, and vie for the attention and affection and approval of others becomes strong and at times even overpowering. It is that life manual that keeps them on track toward that goal of becoming mature and perfected as an adult, which protects them from harmful and even fatal behaviors.

It is in this time that we see some of those juvenile, intense emotionly charged jealousies over boyfriends. These "hormone-charged" feelings bring rage and fights over even the smallest of things. It's in these times that we learn through claiming someone with whom we are infatuated as our turf. They belong to us, and we will so to speak scratch the eyes out of anyone who tries to interfere or steal our beau.

During the time of the Jews settling into the land of Canaan there were many turf wars. While it appeared to be wars over land between all the different people who laid claim to that land, all the nations felt a deeper sense of inheritance and ownership than just the right to exist on it. Genesis 16:12 agreed that Ishmael would be a wild man. When Abraham was about to die in Genesis 25:5, we read that Abraham gave all he had to Isaac. The lineage of Isaac received Abraham's blessing, not the lineage of Ishmael, yet the descendants of Ishmael claimed the land. This is the feuding of adolescents over bragging rights to God and what God gives them—the relationship with God. The land is a secondary issue.

Because adolescents are learning how to get along and behave appropriately with each other, they often have to house arbitration based on what is fair and their rights. It is a trademark of immature behavior. Between Abraham and Moses something was lost among the Ishmaelites. They had Abraham's seed and the promise of God that they would be a great nation. From that point they were left on their own to develop rules to live by that were not given by God. The Israelites, on the other hand, were given the Mosaic laws and the Ten Commandments. Two commandments—thou shalt love the Lord thy God, and thou shall love thy neighbor as thyself—contain a word missing from the Islamic faith and that which sponsored Ishmael. That word is "love."

You see, the most important piece of maturing is in the understanding of love. The Ishmaelites went on to worship God, and do what God wants; they may even feel they love God. However, one cannot love God and hate their brother, 1 John 4:20. What they must then do is relate to God and others through a sense of right and fairness. The only way one can go beyond that juvenile sense of fairness is to know God through Jesus as his spirit of love matures us.

We can only come to the measure of the stature of the fullness of Christ and no more be children tossed to and fro, but grow up into him in all things when we accept Christ as our savior or and believe on him, Ephesians 4:13-16.

CHAPTER 13

Davidic Covenant: Adolescent Teen Years II

1 Corinthians 13:11

*"When I was a child, I spoke as a child, I understood
as a child, I thought as a child: but when I
became a man, I put away childish things."*

In the process of being a girl in the adolescent years, we come to a time when we must put to the test the things we have learned about the boundaries that have been set for us. The determining factor of whether we make a good choice or a bad choice in this test is how well we have translated our lessons into good values.

King David lived about five hundred years after Moses. The children of Israel had settled into the Promised Land and parceled it into two divisions. One is known as Judah and the other as Israel. David becomes king of Judah. He grew up tending his father's sheep. While out in the fields tending the flock, he reads the law and talks with God. He is still just a young man when he is called to take provisions to his brothers who are fighting the Philistines under King Saul.

While there, he is thrust into battle with the largest, meanest, most intimidating man in the Philistine army. You know the story, David kills Goliath, and Saul brings David to the palace to live. David begins to rise in power. Saul becomes jealous. And so the battle between Saul and David begins.

Now David is faced with some choices that will try every piece of faith and knowledge he possesses. David has only that which he has learned from the law, family, and the Lord. He must reach down deep inside and draw on these things to guide him through his trials with Saul. David makes good choices and becomes king. I believe we can get an insight as to why David made good choices at this time.

In Psalms 119:9-16 we read, "*Wherewithal shall a young man plan his way? By taking heed thereto according to thy word. With my whole heart I sought thee: oh, let me not wander from thy commandments. Thy word have I hid in mine heart, that I might not sin against thee. Blessed art thou, O, Lord: teach me thy statutes. With my lips have I declared all the judgments of thy mouth. I have rejoiced in the way of thy testimonies, as much as in all riches. I will meditate in thy precepts and have respect unto thy ways. I will delight myself in thy statutes; I will not forget thy word."*

David made good choices because he placed the things he learned deep within his heart. They became an integral part of him. He connected with God and his values became David's own spiritual guide. The things he learned were not only intellectually in his mind but also became values in his spirit.

David captured the concept of living by values, placed in the heart directly, from God, so God told David that his kingdom would last forever. For over two hundred years, nineteen kings from David's family line rules over Judah. Jesus was in David's lineage and thus David's kingdom would live forever.

David was a man after God's heart. It's easy to understand when you see how David placed the relationship with God in the heart instead of the head. This is what Jesus taught and what the New Testament is about. After the time of David, we read over and over both in the New Testament and finally in Revelations that God wants to be our God and for us to be his people. The entire New Testament speaks to the issue of God in us.

The prophets of the Old Testament wrote with much the same relationship with God as did David. They seem to have captured what David understood. There is a marked increase in maturity and depth of relationship with God from the time of David to the time of Christ, as opposed to the time of Moses to the time of David.

Things were not always rosy after David's reign. In time the children of Judah and Israel were led captive. They had tough times. Most of the books of the prophets were written while the prophets were in captivity. Yet the Israelites were still productive and worshiped God. Even though their temple and the city of Jerusalem were destroyed, they rebuilt it and regained their spiritual identity as a nation devoted to God.

The Bride-To-Be Grows

Through the period of the Davidic covenant, which covers from David to the time of Jesus, we see a marked maturity in the Hebrew people. One could say, well, they broke covenants, so God sent them in captivity. You are right, of course.

I want you to look at this one-thousand-year time period as being not so much a story of man's failures but a recording of the bride's growth.

In our analogy of the bride we see the time of Moses until the time of Jesus as those teen years. The years spent going from puberty into adulthood. There are actually two phases that we go through as people growing up in this time. As we shared in chapter 11, the first phase is learning the principles and rules of living. Now we see in chapter 12 that instead of having them in our mind and trying to behave according to rules, they began to take root and become integrated into our character.

At some point in this maturing process we begin to capture what life is all about. We begin to develop character, a persona, and a value system. This does not always keep us out of trouble because we also test boundaries at this time of our life. All too often we step over the boundaries and have to pay the consequences.

Notice that God did not destroy the children of Israel for their mistakes. Rather he allowed them to suffer the consequences but still loved them as a father loves his child. He did not see their failures and call them hopeless children and choose to destroy them. Instead he promised they would always be his children and he allowed them to grow through their mistakes.

God is raising up a people (a bride-to-be for Christ) by allowing them to grow up even while making mistakes. Therefore as we look at this time period instead of seeing a struggling people being disciplined by God: let us see a heavenly father nurturing this immature child. In his wisdom he is allowing this child to mature to be the perfect bride for Christ.

The Israelites were under tremendous pressure trying to get their maturation right. The other nations (suitors for the God of Abraham's blessing) despised the Israelites. They often held the Israelites captive. God would deliver the Israelites only for them to get into another problem and be held captive by another group.

The typical behavior of an immature person, usually in this age group, is to be held captive by peers and the want of acceptance from the peer group. Because they want to fit in, be accepted, and be part of the group, they do things that are against their better nature and training. Peer pressure, the need to find their identity, and the desire to be independent, overrides parental guidance and other sources of wisdom.

Don't get me wrong, there are many more things involved than just peer pressure. Weighing the child's side in us that demands we have our way without considering any consequences, and the parent side that demands we think only of the wise choices without considering the emotion, is difficult. Making a decision as an adult that accounts for both parent and child opinion and consider safety, and outcome as well as the joy of the experience comes with maturity.

The captivity of the Israelites was not just physical captivity, but during physical captivity there was the discouragement of years and generations of being subjected to poverty, trying to fit in with the other society, and getting along to help with survival. They were emotionally and intellectually held captive by their captor's presence.

Becoming an adult is discovering that freedom comes from the inside. It is learning how to choose friends and relationships without having to be held captive by that other person's beliefs and ideals. It is saying no to destructive relationships even at the cost of offense, and saying yes to healthy and mutually beneficial relationships.

I pastor a small church in Oregon. We do not have a lot of money; we barely meet our budget from month to month. Our church has a missionary program that is very limited, and we would love to do more. Though our church is small we have a big heart and would like to help everybody who comes through those doors.

As the pastor I get requests for financial assistance almost on a daily basis. People want money for a motel, a meal, to fix their car, or to pay a bill. The most common request is by people who say they are passing through town, have a job waiting for them in the next state and just need enough gas or a meal to get them down the road to that job. This occurs as often as two times per week. Often these people try to put pressure on me to give by saying things meant to intimidate me. Sometimes they just demand that I give.

Our church could help every one of these people. We could give everyone something until our money was gone each month. However, we would then soon be unable to pay our utility bills, repair the building, or meet our ministry needs. We could be cynical and choose to give to no one, saving all our money for much wiser uses. We have to make choices.

As adults, our staff and the church put our heads together and choose what charity we will give to and how much we can afford. We consider many things when choosing how we give our money to others in need. We have learned to temper our desire to help with the wisdom to maintain our ability to survive.

We can allow our minds to be held captive because our hearts go out to the needs of so many people. But we must mature to where we can make good decisions meeting the needs as we have ability.

Everybody has needs and desires for something. It is a wonderful thing to listen to people and help where we can and where God calls us to help. When we take this one step further and feel that because someone asks for help, we are obligated to give help. When we feel intimidated into giving and responding accordingly, we are being held captive by those who request. The captivity is truly in our mind. We can say no, and we must say no when we feel that captivity. The only voice to which we must always say yes to is the voice of the Holy Spirit calling us. Anything else is captivity and all captivity is immaturity.

Growing up to be a part of the bride means setting aside all captivity. This bride-to-be for Christ grew through the immaturity of being held captive during that time from Moses to Jesus. Jesus came to set us free from all captivity.

CHAPTER 14

The Church Age: The Adult Emerges and the Groom Pays a Visit

Luke 2:11

"For unto you is born this day in the city of David a Savior, which is Christ our Lord."

The next step of history is known as the Church Age. This officially begins with the resurrection of Jesus. You may have been under the impression that the Church Age started with the birth of Jesus or the very first part of the New Testament. However, salvation came to us with the cross and eternal life came to us with the resurrection of Christ. Therefore, the time that Jesus lived on earth was during the Mosaic dispensation.

To recap: From the time of Moses to the time of the end of the Old Testament, God established the Jewish people. They became known as the Jews both by their faith and their lineage through Isaac. There is a time gap between the book of Malachi and the book of Matthew of four hundred years. This is regarded as the dry time or time of silence or the time of no open vision. There are many recorded writings during this period but none are accepted in the King James Bible or by most Protestant Christian theologians.

At the end of this time of no revelations from God, John the Baptist arose proclaiming himself to be, a voice in the wilderness. It was he who, in the Jordan River, baptized Jesus proclaiming him to be the son of God. It was confirmed by the Holy Spirit descending upon him in the form of a dove. From that day forward the focus is on the ministry of Jesus.

Throughout all of time, from the day Adam was created to this very minute that you are reading this book, there has been no one like Jesus. God promised Adam and Eve, on the outskirts of the garden, that someday his seed would get even with the seed of the serpent. That was about 4,000 years before Jesus would be born. Over the 4,000-year time span over 332 statements regarding Jesus are made in the Bible. They regarded the child, Jesus, would live with them, his birth, and that he would be light, how he would teach, and even his death and resurrection. Jesus fulfilled all the prophecies concerning him on this earth. This can be said of no other person who has ever lived.

Jesus was born of a virgin named Mary. As prophesied he died on a cross, was resurrected in three days, and went to heaven by ascension. No other person on earth has done that, ever. Jesus was born through the family of Noah, Abraham, Isaac, David, and his mother Mary was in David's lineage. While Jesus was born to Mary thus becoming a Jew, he was also the son of God thus becoming deity. No other person can make that claim.

Jesus, one of the three personages of God, ended an era of law and obedience to God. As I shared earlier, it became one of relationship and responsibility between God and man. In his life Jesus demonstrated through teaching and practice how that relationship between him and his church should be lived out in each of us. In Revelations 19, God likens Jesus to being the groom and the church being the bride. Jesus died as the lamb, sacrificed to God for our sins.

From the time of Adam until the time of Christ an animal was sacrificed for sin. That ended with Jesus, signifying that whoever believed on him would have everlasting life, John 3:16.

In Matthew 5:17, Jesus states that he did not come to destroy the law but to fulfill the *law*. This means that the intent of the law stayed in place even though it was impossible for anyone to live their life and fully comply with the entire law. Jesus never ended the intent of the law. His life was a demonstration of how we can also fulfill the law.

The way the law is fulfilled is to allow Christ in us to accomplish what the law cannot. It is not from knowledge or discipline, but rather from a new heart and being changed into the likeness of Christ.

It was the intent and purpose of Jesus to show us how to live, and that we would live accordingly. So often it is said that he was the son of God, and we can't live up to his standard. Yet we read in Ephesians 4:13, which say that we all should come into the unity of the faith, and knowledge of the son of God, to a perfect man, unto the measure of the stature of the fullness of Christ.

To those of us who believe the Scripture is the infallible word of God: we must recognize this verse never says we must try to become a perfect man on to the measure of the stature of the fullness of Christ. It explicitly says "until *we all come.*"

This is a key Scripture in the Bible and a pivotal Scripture in man's history; and should be a cornerstone, a foundation, and a fundamental doctrine in Christian life. You see, Jesus is looking for a bride who is equal to him. Through the first four books of the New Testament we get a glimpse of what that means. We see the life of Jesus and how he lived and related to the heavenly father. This then becomes our standard for relationship with Jesus and the Father.

You may say yes, but that was two thousand years ago, or nobody is perfect, or that particular Scripture refers to when we get to heaven.

The rest of this book is dedicated to when the bride is perfected, how the bride is perfected, and what that perfection or *fullness of the stature of Christ* will look like when it comes.

Now let's look at the bride-to-be and the reaction of their first introduction to the groom. Let's go back and quickly review the growth of the bride to this point as shared in the previous chapters.

The birth of the bride began with Adam and Eve. They were formed by God and developed in the womb of the Garden of Eden. They were expelled from the garden when they disobeyed God.

The baby phase was learning to walk after the fall from the garden; the toddler phase is seen as they grow through the time of Adam through Noah, covered in the book of Genesis.

Shortly after the flood and the Tower of Babel, Abraham appears on the scene. The time from Abraham until the time Moses received the Ten Commandments and the law on Mount Sinai could be seen as a time of early childhood.

The child enters into those early adolescent years with the advent of the law and the Exodus from Egypt. It is demonstrated throughout the Old Testament up until the time Jesus comes.

The four hundred years that transpires between the Old Testament (Malachi to Matthew) and the New Testament could be likened to the time when an adolescent turns eighteen and the time they become responsible for themselves in their home or maybe off to college. It's like the time when we go from dependency on our parents to complete independence from them. It is a transitional and hopefully short period of time.

So we find that the time Christ was on this earth was literally a time when the Jews cross paths with the son of God. But in our analogy, it is the bride of Christ, as a young woman, crossing paths with him who would eventually become her groom. The Jews were looking for a Messiah. They even asked Jesus if he was the Messiah. Obviously they recognize Jesus as someone very special. They just could not recognize that he was the chosen one, the Messiah, their Savior, the groom-to be.

You know how it is, growing up, reaching eighteen years of age, where you felt you were an adult in every sense of the word. You were out from under parental authority, being your person; you dated to find that special someone to come into your life as a spouse. And then you found the person who you thought was that special one. Remember how you felt? Perhaps you were unsure and not quite ready for commitment of that magnitude. Perhaps you were even scared.

Well, this is probably similar to the way the people were feeling as they heard about their special someone coming. All the prophets had been talking about it, the priest were still laying out the rules of protocol for their Messiah.

Kind of like us as we wait for the entrance of our special someone. We practice manners, personal hygiene, being reliable, looking and acting just right. Like us, the people of the Old Testament and in the day of Jesus's coming were eagerly looking for their special someone: God to be specific. They must have wondered what he would look like, how we will know him, how are we going to be in his presence, and will he bring a better life? Will there be fewer problems and more resources in my life because he came into it?

Then he arrives! Well, not quite what they expected. He arrived as a baby! Thus begins their next phase of growing. You've heard the story. Jesus was so different from the family of the bride-to-be that it caught them by surprise. He seemed to be out of tune with their concept of what the Messiah would be. He said these foreign and scary things that were outside the realm of normal conversation or even imagination by the very ones he came to court. They found him just too different, so they sent him on his way and decided to look for another.

But wait! There's more. There was a remnant that listened to what Jesus said. They believed in him. Through this small group known as the apostles, a seed-of-faith group that flourished over the years into what we know as the church. When Jesus ascended into heaven the church became known as his body. He was no longer on earth in physical form, and we are the embodiment of all that Jesus was on earth.

If we relate this body to the bride of Christ, this would be the time that the bride meets the groom-to-be and begins to fall in love.

Somewhat unsure of what this means and what the groom really wants, the bride (the church) begins to work on personal issues so that she might be compatible to this man she loves. If we look at the church from the time of Christ's departure and the day of Pentecost, until the time of the last days, we can easily see how the church is grooming itself for the acceptance and approval of Jesus and his father. It is just like the children of Israel looking for the Messiah when Jesus came the first time.

A brief courtship of Jesus and the church while he walked the face of this earth was enough to change the entire character makeup of his bride. His kindness, love, faith, understanding, and ability to communicate were above anything any other leader of people ever possessed. He performed miracles that transformed not only the body but the heart and soul of man. We beheld him but could not esteem him appropriately because his ways and thoughts were so far more mature than ours. There had never been anyone who could measure up to his depth and stature.

The most important thing that the bride discovered about this man Jesus was that he was not interested in having an arranged marriage or a relationship based on rules of behavior. He did not play the games of the Pharisees by trying to manipulate the law and still gain favor with God. Jesus was interested in a personal relationship with his chosen love and bride-to-be that would last for eternity and is based on love, truth, and faith with a completely open communication.

This completely changed the way the bride would relate to God and her beloved, Jesus.

As we look at the growth cycle of the bride at this time, we have to recognize that something amazing finally becomes a reality in the maturing process. To this point the relationship between the bride and God was governed by games of trying to define rules and getting away with selfish motivated behaviors, keeping personal feelings quite secret, and leaving the options open to back out of personal situations. Now the relationship between the bride and God is governed by openness, honesty, and love and is driven by a commitment to the relationship.

The relationship that Jesus brought to his people while on the earth was the introduction of a relationship of intimacy, vulnerability, and commitment. This new level of intimacy cannot be experienced by a juvenile, mentally immature, or spiritually undeveloped person. His maturity brings the ultimate experience in intimacy and can only be experienced when we become as mature as Christ, Ephesians 5:13.

At the point of Jesus appearing, and even his ascension, the bride was nowhere near the maturity of Christ. I believe that because of this disparity, the Jews, who represented the bride to that point, could not understand or perceive what he was all about. Consequently, like a young woman who is not ready for the mature relationship and intimacy that leads to marriage, finds a man who is much more mature to be so foreign and scary that she is unable to connect and therefore rejects him as a possible suitor.

The Jews rejected Christ. Jesus found the bride he was looking for through a remnant of Jews and a collection of Gentiles who come together and said Jesus is the one. They accepted, embraced, and completely committed themselves to growing into the perfect and acceptable bride of Christ.

Did this first group of believers in Christ have it all figured out? No! Did they understand him fully and where it was going to lead for generations and generations later? Probably not. Like any single person they grew, and their growth was but a short span of growth in the long life of the bride. It is good to remember that the bride of Christ was born six thousand years ago. If birth was with Adam and the wedding marks full maturity in Christ, which many believe could happen any day, then the time Jesus walked on this earth marks that young adulthood when the bride-to-be is just discovering and courting the groom-to be.

The early church had to experience Christ through the Holy Spirit. Through the experience of walking with Jesus, this set the foundation for a relationship of discovery and growing close that will carry through until the wedding.

What about the Jews?

Jesus was rejected by the mass of the Jewish people. They rejected him as their Messiah. Their belief is that the Messiah will come and deliver them and they will reign with him forever. They are correct in their beliefs to this extent: he will if they accept Jesus. Unfortunately, they expected Jesus to deliver them physically, from their enemies, while he lived on earth. God's plan to bring them their Messiah is still in the future. While God still has a place in his heart and in his plans for them as special people we must remember, and they must recognize that to be part of the bride they must recognize the groom.

Do you recall that we talked about Ishmael chapter 10 and the children of Ishmael becoming another suitor to the groom? They wanted the blessing of the bride-to-be but were not willing to become what the groom sought. Now they and the Jews fall into that same category. They want to claim all of God's blessings but reject his son: and therefore cannot be a part of that bride. They must confess Jesus as the Son of God and do what all of us must do; love him and grow in to that mature relationship to the equal stature of the fullness of Christ.

CHAPTER 15

The Groom Writes Love Letters

1 John 4:16

"And we have known and believed the love that God hath to us. God is love; and he that dwells in love dwells in God, and God in him."

The Facts

Through the life of the apostles, about forty years after the resurrection of Jesus, many people came to know Jesus as their personal savior and took up their cross and followed him. They become a part of this great movement called Christianity. Churches are established and the word is dispersed from Jerusalem to Rome, from Ethiopia to Turkey, and from Greece to Persia.

The gospel is spread by word-of-mouth. It traveled quite rapidly and great numbers of people were converted. There was no radio, TV, Internet, Facebook, Twitter, or telephone. There were people sharing the good news by word-of-mouth from person to person. The news spreads fast. People were converted to Jesus at a phenomenal rate. Churches sprang up from Jerusalem through Greece, Turkey, and the entire Roman empire.

People traveled by foot or rode animals. Their boats had oars or sails, no motors. Their mode of transportation was much slower than it is today. Even written letters were sent by carriers on horses or by friends on foot.

In a time when news traveled so slow that it could take years to even hear about a big event like an earthquake, this news, these events of the new church had such a dynamic impact; it changed so many people's entire lives in such a short time that it was phenomenal. There had to be something more than a simple sharing of the Word such as "Did you hear what happened in Israel?"

It all started in the upper room as described in the second chapter of Acts. One hundred twenty people were filled with the Holy Ghost. They spoke in tongues, were endued with power, and were in one accord in this upper room. They left that room empowered and exuberant. So much so that people outside gathered around and asked what great thing was going on upstairs? The spread of the gospel (good news) started on that day when Peter explained to the onlookers the event they had just witnessed and said to them to "repent and be baptized for the remission of their sins." Three thousand people were saved that day, many of whom were from foreign countries.

From that day, everywhere the apostles went, they would speak to people of the power of Jesus to change lives. People believed and received Christ and were dynamically transformed into a new kind of person.

I suppose we could try to find all kinds of natural explanations for that rapid spread of the gospel. Critics would love to be able to explain away with rationales that sound good but ignore the truth of what really happened at that time. But for those who believe the answer is simple, there really is only one explanation.

In Acts 1:8, Jesus says, *"You shall receive power, after that the Holy Ghost is come upon you: and you shall be witnesses to Me both in Jerusalem, and in all Judea, and in Samaria, and to the outermost part of the Earth."* This is what happened on the day of Pentecost and continued to happen daily for the apostles and new believers.

In John 14:16-17, Jesus says, *"I will pray the Father, and He shall give you another comforter, that He may abide with you forever; even the Spirit of truth; whom the world cannot receive, because it sees Him not, neither knows Him: but you know Him for He dwells with you, and He shall be in you."* The disciples, who were in the upper room, were filled with the Holy Spirit and the Holy Spirit dwelled in them from that day on. This was a new experience which changes the life of everyone who experiences it.

In John 14:26, Jesus says, *"The comforter, which is the Holy Ghost, whom the father will send in my name, He shall teach you all things, and bring all things to your remembrance whatsoever I have said to you. "* From the day the disciples received the Holy Spirit, he became their teacher. We must always remember that the Holy Spirit is a he, one of the triune Godhead, and not an *it*. He is an entity who is alive. He is not a concept, a conglomeration of ideas, a perception of our mind, or an imagined force. He is God as much as Jesus is God. He is God as much as our heavenly father is God. They are three and yet they are one.

The phenomenon of the gospel being spread by the apostles is straightforward. It was not by their power or abilities that people's lives were changed. It was by the work of the Holy Spirit in their lives, empowering their words with his conviction that spoke to others causing them to accept Jesus as their savior. *"God commended His love toward us, in that, while we were yet sinners, Christ died for us"* (Romans 5:8). People were converted because of the Holy Spirit's conviction. They experienced Jesus's love, which changed their lives.

What Really Happened

What happened to the thousands and thousands of people who walked with Jesus in the streets, who were fed by him miraculously, who were healed by him, who witnessed the healing of others such as Lazarus, the blind man, and the woman with the issue of blood? Where did those people go? Where were they when the Holy Spirit came to those in the upper room? Of the tens of thousands of people who knew Jesus and his teachings, only a small handful of 120 people met in a small upper chamber room on that historically changing day at the feast of Pentecost. What was so different between the 120 and the tens of thousands of others who witnessed the same things?

It would be trite, to say the least, that the Holy Spirit was poured out on the day of Pentecost on 120 people and that's what changed them. Even though that's the facts, there's more to the story than just believing in a cause. Something new occurred in these 120 people that did not occur in all the rest or anyone else up to that point in time. While the 120 people believed on Jesus before Pentecost, it was only on this day that they underwent a dramatic change in their entire character.

Oh, Happy Day

On this day, they experienced new life, not just increased knowledge about Jesus. They experienced their sins being forgiven, washed away forever. It was not just words that describe the event. They felt their burden of guilt and shame of the wrong doings of the past, that the blood of bulls and goats could not take away, lifted from their heart and back; in place a robe of righteousness wrapped about them by the Spirit of God.

The drudgery and sadness of being in a rut in life without hope gave way to the exhilaration of being in the presence of God and the reality of eternal life

Their lack of sense of purpose greater than themselves, and what could be accomplished on this earth, gave way to faith in a purpose and plan that stretched beyond themselves into eternity with Jesus. Their hollow religion became a life-giving experience. Now Jesus was not gone from them, but instead, a savior was born to them.

The old ways became new ways. Demanding fairness fell aside to forgiveness. Turmoil of bickering over dogma was replaced by the peace of acceptance. Sorrows fled as God's joy filled their hearts. Attacking others for their shortcomings and wrongdoings received no attention for now there was complete acceptance. Love came in place of hate. And the presence of a loving God replaced fear of reprisal for wrongdoing.

With love in their hearts, faith in God because of the presence of the Holy Spirit, and the hope of being in the presence of God for ever, they embarked on a new love life, sharing the good news of Jesus and inviting everyone to be reborn just as they had been on that day.

Are you beginning to get a picture of a woman who discovers the man of her dreams and finds that he is everything she always wanted? She gets excited, has to share it with all of her friends, and is inherently full of joy. She has total faith, seeing only the wonderful and delightful life her future holds. This is the way a person feels when they find Jesus as their savior. This is also the way the new Christians felt as they begin to experience salvation, something they had never even heard of before.

Although Jesus had ascended to heaven and was only with us for a short time, he left the church (the bride-to-be) with two things. He left them with the Holy Spirit and his love letters.

When a person gives his life to Jesus and invites him in to be the savior and lord of his life, he comes in as well as the Holy Spirit. The Holy Spirit is that part of the Godhead who can reside within people as well as moved upon the face of the earth at the same time. He is omnipresent. It is he who lights up his people and gives them the confidence that Jesus will return to claim them as part of his bride. It is through the Holy Spirit that we believe that Jesus lives within us. All who receive Jesus as their savior are groomed by the Holy Spirit and are guided into the likeness of Jesus so that they will be of equal stature with him upon his return.

The Love Letters

The second thing he left us was his love letters. He inspired his apostles and others to write letters and record what he wished to say to those he left behind. I would like to think that they were the love letters sent to his beloved. The couriers were the apostles, prophets, and holy men of old who scribed them. The Holy Spirit is the courier who brings the letters to us and brings them alive.

Is it any wonder that the people on this earth, who are not part of that special bride-to-be, cannot understand or even appreciate what he said to them in his letters?

But to us, who are in love with Jesus and have found eternal life through him, these same words are life. We sift through them repeatedly gleaning new bits of insight to our beloved. As we grow older and more mature, we find new and hidden meaning when we read these love letters. Is it any wonder that we, who have discovered this wonderful relationship with Jesus, read his love letters over and over, receiving new hope and insight to our Lord?

The closer we get to the time of his return, and the more we read our love letters, the more the Holy Spirit reveals the meaning behind the words. Like King David of old we read these words and hide them in our hearts, counting them precious revelations of our beloved.

Many people wrote about Jesus's life, death, resurrection, and ascension. There were many, many letters and writings about the early church fathers and how the gospel was spread in the AD first century. These writings were not compiled into one complete work for centuries to come. The gospel was handed down by word-of-mouth. The written documentation of Christ was preserved by different people and not shared at large with the masses.

The bride grew through inspired people, sharing repeated stories of Jesus and the apostles and through faith in God based on their experience of salvation and miracles that continued to happen through the centuries. It is important to remember that the Jews who rejected Jesus did not have that same phenomenon occurring as the new believers. They did not see the miracles, they did not add greatly to their numbers, their faith did not change thousands and thousands of people's lives. The Jews went on about their business as usual.

The Ishmaelites and other religions did not have a great revival. Their lives went on with business as usual. They also saw no miracles.

CHAPTER 16

The Five Suitors

1 John 4:1

"Beloved, believe not every spirit, but try the spirits whether they are of God: because many false prophets are gone out into the world."

From the time of Noah until the Tower of Babel civilization primarily collected and stayed together. People attempted to reach out to God by building a tower that would reach up to heaven. God dispersed the people from that point because he did not want them to build the tower. He obviously knew that would be a hopeless and endless effort.

The people dispersed across the world over the next roughly three thousand years. And the people populated the earth. As the populations grew over that period of time, there became five distinct ways in which people related to God. The ways people related to God were different among clans, tribes, and geographical areas. As time progressed individuals developed their theologies and created groups based around those ideologies.

While each one of the five different types grew they developed their way of dealing with God. They developed their theology, philosophies, sense of government, and methods of growing their theology. Some involved God and some did not. Some groups became aggressive and even evil. Other groups were passive and content to be left alone. While yet a third method of living was to share the goodness and freedom, which they discovered from God, with others.

This was a time when people were learning about themselves and God. It was a time of learning how to get along with others and what they themselves were all about.

In relationship to the growth time of a human being is the time from entering puberty to the time of being on their own as young adults. If we could relate to all the struggles that we have as people we could get an insight to what society went through over these years.

Take a moment to think about how you struggled to learn and adjust to the world in which you had to live. As we find our way through the educational and growth years we develop from a dependent person into an independant person who can survive in a harsh cruel world on our own. It involves many contests that pit you and your strength against others in their strength. We vie for first place in these contests be it the first or the second chair in an orchestra, the valedictory honor at school, the best in the sport that we chose, or the best job being offered. Life is full of contests.

Such was this time period. In the next five chapters we will discuss all five of the types of people that evolved. We must remember that in spite of their feuds and wars, underneath it all was the quest for God. People have a basic inner drive to be at peace with their god, whether it be a god they created or to discover the god that created them.

CHAPTER 17

Christians: The Bride

John 13:35

"By this shall all men know that you are my disciples, if you have love one to another."

Christians: Another Name for the Bride

By AD 100, Jesus has returned to heaven, the Holy Spirit is given to the world and poured out on the apostles, and the apostles have now all died. What is left behind for the budding church of Jesus is a large group of letters written by the apostles, memories and stories of their ministry, and a large number of people who have come together believing in Jesus as the returning Messiah.

The church was not left alone. The Holy Spirit moved on the hearts of those who would believe the gospel of Jesus Christ. The letters began to be collected and reproduced and spread to Europe, parts of Asia, and parts of Africa as well in the Middle East.

As the church grew and flourished its constituents were given the name Christians. They were followers of Christ. They seem to have a unique and the winning way about them. They preached and taught that salvation came through Jesus Christ and his crucifixion. They shared a common belief that Jesus died and rose again and ascended to heaven and that he would someday return and take them all to heaven to be with him.

People who lived in Europe and Asia and northern Africa were not familiar with the story of Jesus. The news was spread by word-of-mouth in converts to this newfound faith. It spread from community to community. It changed people's morals, values, and consequently, the way they practiced their lives. It then began changing the way people practiced community government. Communities raised up churches, which became the center for guidance in community lives.

The church increased. It began to push into all of Europe, the Middle East, and northern Africa, converting people to Christianity. By AD 1000 the church was well entrenched in society.

Unfortunately, there was constant change and turmoil. The church suffered persecution from nonbelievers, who felt threatened by its influence upon people they wished to control.

In our analogy of the church being the bride of Christ, this time period is similar to that of a young woman entering adulthood and establishing her life.

Much like in the Song of Solomon, the romance with the beloved begins. When Jesus came to earth he courted his bride, they spent time together, and the bride learned all about her beloved. As short as the time seemed to be that Christ was on earth, there was a great impact and influence of him on the bride-to-be.

Then the time came that Jesus had to leave. He told his beloved that he had to go away and that he would prepare a place for them to live forever, together happily ever after. As mentioned in the last chapter he wrote love letters to the church through his couriers the apostles. He also reminded his betrothed that his spirit, his very essence would be with her to comfort her and remind her of his return. He shared that this comforter would guide her in becoming exactly what he was looking for in a bride.

In those years from the time Jesus left until around AD 1000, the bride grew and became strong and independent. Doubters and scoffers would share very ugly accusations and say that Jesus was a myth and that he would never return because he was dead. This only caused the bride to grow stronger. She was beaten by the Romans, chastised by the Jews, despised by others, and Ishmaelites tried to rob her of her Messiah, the coming one.

Through all this she survived and even grew stronger. She read the love letters, searching them, studying them, and living in those words as they became real and alive to her. The Holy Spirit spoke to her heart and developed character and made her different from the rest of the world. She became such a dynamic influence that others looking upon her feared her because members of their selfish "churches" were being converted and changed to be a part of this bride.

The more people tried to destroy the bride the stronger she became, overcoming the opposition shown toward her. While she was not perfect and made many mistakes, she kept growing stronger and stronger in the image of her beloved that the letters described and the spirit portrayed.

Jesus told his followers that all that he went through, they too would go through. His bride would suffer rejection and persecution from the other suitors just as he had suffered while he was on this earth.

CHAPTER 18

The Jews

John 1:11

"He came unto his own, and His own received Him not."

When a famine came to the land of Abraham, Jacob, his grandson took all of the Israelites to Egypt because Joseph had gained favor with Pharaoh and had plenty of food for them. The Israelites lived four hundred years in Egypt. They fell into slavery to the Egyptians and became abused and down-trodden people until Moses brought deliverance to them. Moses led them out of Egypt and returned them to Canaan, which was the promised land of Abraham.

I must interject here that when the Israelites left Egypt they stopped at Sinai. Here Moses receives the law and the tablets of the Ten Commandments from God. God establishes an order for the nation of Israel that covers government, social life, spiritual life, and how they deal with other nations and people. God spoke directly with Moses to establish the Jewish people as an organized nation.

When they arrived at Canaan under the leadership of Joshua, they were met with much resistance. The Jews came to reclaim the land they left. It had been four hundred years since they left and other tribes, including the Ishmaelites, had settled into that land. They viewed it as an abandoned land, which became theirs. Is it any wonder that the Ishmaelites and the Israelites fought over the land from that day until the present time?

This is where we clearly see the conflict between three of the suitors for God: the fight over the land they both wish to occupy. They were Israelites, Ishmaelites, and other tribes that were not of Abraham's family and some who were Abraham's descendants but not of Isaac or Ishmael.

We have been covering the Israelites because they were the lineage that created Jesus. They were parts of the bride until Jesus rose from the dead and went to heaven. As we have shared, from the time of Jesus's ascension to heaven, the bride became those who were followers of him known as Christians

The Jews who rejected Christ and maintained their belief in God believe that Jesus was a prophet but not the Son of God. Yet they cling to God and look for their Messiah to come and rescue them someday. They look for eternal life with him. They look for a time when he'll establish his kingdom among the Jews, and they shall reign forever. It is this author's opinion that because they were blessed through Isaac and produced Jesus they will have a special place in God's plan. They may not experience the rapture and be in a part of the bride as we Christians believe is to come. However, God will honor their part to play in the making of the bride. They clearly have a place in the heart of God and an eternal presence with him and us.

Because they worship the one true God, the God of Abraham, they become suitors to God's particular and special blessing. They feel their faith in God and their obedience to him grants them the privilege of being the ones that God will favor in the end. While Christians and Jews have great fellowship and kinship, there is still a disagreement about the love letters and the validity of the coming of the eternal prince of peace.

The Jews yet hold to their claim of God's special blessing to them, and their faith that he will send a Messiah for them. This makes them suitors for God's special blessing.

From the time of enslavement by Egypt until 1948, Israel has been in and out of captivity. They have been accepted and blessed by some nations: primarily those with the Christian foundations. They have been rejected and persecuted by other nations. Most Christian scholars view the return of Israel to its homeland in 1948 as a significant point in time signaling the last days. We'll talk more about this in later chapters.

CHAPTER 19

The Ishmaelites or the Muslims

Genesis 25:6

"Unto the sons of the concubines, which Abraham happened, Abraham gave gifts, and sent them away from Isaac his son, while he yet lived, eastward, unto the east country."

True to human nature, when a young lady meets prince charming and others see the beauty and greatness in their relationship, jealousy occurs. The bride was experiencing something greater than had ever happened on earth. No other person (collective group) had anything near what the bride was experiencing.

The Muslims are just such a group. They saw the wonder of Christ and wanted him to be theirs.

Ishmael was the firstborn son of Abraham. Ishmael was born to Hagar, Sarah's handmaid. Isaac was the second born son. Isaac received the blessing of God because he was the promised one from Sarah, Abraham's wife. We have read about this in chapter 10 of this book and the book of Genesis. Ishmael and his descendants become one of the suitors to the prince of peace. The Israelites became one of the suitors to the prince of peace. Let's take a look at the latter of these two suitors from the time of Abraham until about AD 1000.

The Ishmaelites group grew in numbers and began to spread their family out into Europe and North Africa as well as the Middle East. From the time of Abraham's death until the time of Christ there was no one central belief system among Ishmael's descendants. The two main points they hung onto were that they were the descendants of Abraham, and therefore have the blessing of Abraham's God whom they call Allah; and that they deserved to have the land that Abraham possessed.

In the previous chapter we shared how the Israelite's went to Egypt. In the meantime the Ishmaelites govern themselves by each tribe or community with self-government. In fact, the Christian faith infiltrated the faith of the Ishmaelites. While they did not become clear-cut Christians, they did adopt the belief that Jesus (Isa) was an important prophet. They believed that he was born miraculously by the virgin Mary. They believe that Jesus was not crucified but ascended to heaven and will return to earth near that great Day of Judgment to restore justice and defeat the false messiah also known as the antichrist. They believe he will return with some Muslims for the Islam people. These beliefs are held by the Muslims, the Islamic people today.

While they held to their faith in Abraham's God, they had no central figure to guide them until Muhammad came on the scene around AD 570. The Koran, the sacred words of Mohammed, is considered to be the final word of God to the Muslims because Mohammed was the last great prophet and the greatest of all.

Mohammed lived in Mecca and Medina and the words of the Koran are the wisdom's that he shared with others. They were later put into a script called the Koran. It was here that Mohammed developed something similar to what God did through Moses with the law. He organized his local community with an integration of government, social life, and spiritual life. Because of his great success in organizing people and settling disputes, his words became the law. This caught on with the Muslims and Islam became united.

This success spread rapidly into Europe, Africa, and the Middle East and served to organize the Islamic movement. This was the catalyst that made them strong and powerful. This also defined them as a suitor to the blessings of God.

The Islamic people believe that Allah, the God of Abraham, has chosen them as the only way to ascend to God and that he will send Jesus back as a Muslim to deliver them, and they will be supreme above all other people.

Jesus said that he was the way, the truth, the life, the door, and that nobody could enter the kingdom of God except through him. He was not a savior only to the Jews but according to John 3:16, he was also a savior to whosoever believed in him.

While Christians believe that, the Muslims believe he was a prophet and Mohammed was greater. Mohammed's writings (the Koran) are considered holy but not the writings of the New Testament. Yet they become a suitor because they believe Jesus will come back a Muslim. Jesus was not an Ishmaelite nor was he a Muslim.

The Islamic held belief is that of Ishmael. In Genesis, God called Ishmael a wild man whose hand would be against all others and all others' hands would be against him. This suitor is willing to fight and take lives to win their prince.

Chapter 20

The People with the Designer God

John 10:1

"Verily, verily, I say unto you, he that enters not by the door into the sheepfold, but climbs up some other way, the same is a thief and a robber."

John 10:9

"I am the door: by me if any man enter in, he shall be saved."

The fourth suitor to God is the one that Paul talked about in Acts 17. There Paul stood on Mars Hill and addressed the people's devotion to "the unknown god." Since the Tower of Babel, when God dispersed people around the earth, there have been those who lost their way and understanding of God. They were not the lost tribes of Israel, but they were the lost tribes. They dispersed around the earth. Some even settled in the Middle East.

It is all of these people, who, left to their thinking and no guidance at all from God, created the belief in *"the God as you know him to be."*

Over decades, centuries, and millenniums without a revelation from God, people have worshipped God in a way they could imagine him to be and/or want him to be. This is why there are so many images of God around the earth. There is the god of the sun, god of the moon, a rain god, and even a fertility god. Some folks even believe God is a concept. Something that God is made up of everybody and everything and, consequently, we are part of God. Some believe there is a god but he is comprised of our energy. The Greeks and the Romans had many, many gods.

All of these gods and concepts of God, and there are literally thousands and thousands, are addressed in one statement Paul made concerning the unknown god. They do not know or understand God and, consequently, worship God's expression toward mankind or this earth. We see these people even today. You can identify them through some of their favorite sayings.

"I don't have to go to church to find God. I feel closer to God out in the woods than I do in church. Christians are a bunch of hypocrites. God is in everything and everybody. We are all children of God. I use the alignment of stars, planets, and dates and times for God to reveal things to me. I read tarot cards and I'm in touch with spirits who guide me. There are many paths to God. If you are one with the universe you are one with God. I worship God in my own way. I do not need to be in church or with other Christians to worship God."

Here's what the apostle Paul says in the book of Romans.

"Because that, when they knew God, they glorified Him not as God, neither were thankful; but became vain in their imaginations, and their foolish heart was darkened. Professing their selves to be wise, they became fools, and changed the glory of the un-corruptible God into an image made like to corruptible man, and to birds, and four-footed beasts, and creeping things.

Wherefore God also gave them up to uncleanliness through the lusts of their own hearts, to dishonor their own bodies between themselves: who changed the truth of God into a lie and worshiped and served the creature more than the creator, who is blessed forever.

For this cause God gave them up unto vile affections: for even their women did change the natural use into that which is against nature: and likewise also the men leaving the natural use of the woman, burned in their lust one toward another; men with men working that which is unseemly, and receiving in themselves that recompense of their error which was meet.

And even as they did not like to retain God in their knowledge, God gave them over to a reprobate mind, to do those things which are not convenient; being filled with all unrighteousness, fornication, wickedness, covetousness, maliciousness; full of envy, murder, debate, deceit,

malignity, whisperers, back biters, haters of God, despite
full, proud, boasters, inventors of evil things, disobedient
to parents, without understanding, covenant breakers,
without natural affection, implacable, unmerciful: who
knowing the judgment of God, that they which commit
such things are worthy of death, not only do the same, but
have pleasure in them that do them. "Romans 1:21-32

This is a theistic movement that began with the disbursement of the people at the Tower of Babel. Over many centuries and millenniums this movement has grown quite large in number primarily because it is the easy road, but that still leaves a person to feel justified. Paul describes it as the road that leads to destruction.

To paraphrase that Scripture in today's language it would be said something like this.

When the people, who were at the Tower of Babel, knew God but did not honor him as God by doing what he wanted nor were they thankful to him for what he provided to them were scattered, they lost contact with God. They used their self as images and imagined God would be like what they were. In so doing they worshiped the creature God made and the creation he made but did not worship him. They could not worship him because they had no concept of what he was or wanted.

Without God's spirit guiding and leading them they became lost and void of purpose. They became so lost they could not even remember or imagine what God was like and therefore lost complete contact with him. When this happened they resorted to doing whatever they thought was good for them to do. It doesn't take a genius to read the last few verses in Romans for one to figure out the description of these people.

This group of people, the polytheistic worshipers and the many-roads-to-God believers, has a more subtle way of dealing with Christians, Muslims, and Jews. They just include everybody and say the Abrahamic-God people are just another way. Therefore, their belief is that we all will ascend to God in our own way. The Buddhists, Hindus, and many individual tribal groups follow a path that includes a form of god worship but never connects with the God of Abraham. The hereafter may be through reincarnation in that one comes back as a better person with higher power or a lesser person with lower power, depending on their behavior here on earth.

When the children of Israel returned to Canaan, they spent many decades fighting with the people who inhabited that land. Instead of fighting with some, they chose to cohabitate and get along with the people that were there. Many of these people had multiple gods and barbaric practices in worshiping their gods. The Israelites chose not to fight and instead joined in worshiping strange gods along with their God, even though God clearly told them not to fraternize with those groups in order to protect them from falling into idol worship.

In Exodus 15 we read the song of Moses. This is the song of the redeemed. Israel had been delivered from Egypt and was safe on the other side of the Red Sea from Pharaoh's military. Moses sings of how great God was to deliver them from tyranny and how he would take care of them in the time to come.

As they camped in the land of Marrah, they discovered the water was unfit to drink. The Lord showed Moses a tree that would sweeten the water, so Moses cut down the tree and put it in the water. The water was made sweet. There, on that spot, God gave Moses his first direction for the children of Israel.

Exodus 15:26, "And He said, if thou wilt diligently hearken to the voice of the Lord thy God, and will do that which is right in His sight, and will give ear to His Commandments, and keep all His statutes, I will put none of these diseases upon you, which I have brought upon the Egyptians: for I am the Lord that healeth thee."

The Egyptians did not worship our God, the God of Abraham. They worshiped many gods that they created from their mind. God makes only one condition. To do what is right in *his* sight. Not what is right in their sight. This precluded developing a form of worship of God that mixed anything that did not come from him into their faith. From this time on until they entered the promised land, the land of Canaan (Israel), when they did what God told them, they were successful.

In Judges 17, we see a different picture. A man named Micah tried to be a just and religious person. That word religious, which is improperly used today, means that he had a form of exalting a higher power and not recognizing the one true God. He worshiped Baal and Ashtoreth. They were the pagan god and goddess of the area.

One day along comes a young Levite priest looking for a place to serve God. Micah hires this unnamed priest to be a priest for him. There is one small detail. The priest had to serve and lift up the gods of Micah as well as his God. The Levite priest agrees.

One would gasp and ask how he could do that? Didn't he learn in rabbi school to serve the one true God only?

Judges 17:6 we find the answer.

Judges 17:6, "In those days there was no king in Israel, but every man did that which was right in his own eyes."

This is the beginning of a culture that has grown over the centuries into a massive number. These are people who accept no leadership or authority over their lives unless it agrees with them. They want God, but they can't accept him for who he is, what he wants from us, and the rules he lays down for us to live by. Therefore they create their own rules and become the one who decides what is right in their judgment.

You see, without authority people get lost and caught up in doing what they think is right. They want to be right with God and do what he says; they just decide that God always agrees with them.

This poor young Levite did what was right in his eyes. He saw no harm in participating in the pagan worship of Baal and Ashtoreth. He worshiped God, and his family of Levites learned to live with people of other religions and accommodate their worship of gods and goddesses. Left to his mind and decisions, he made choices that led him into trouble and away from God.

He forgot about what God had told Moses and the children of Israel upon entering the land of Canaan. God told them not to mix with other religions or take up residency with people who had other religions. They were to be a separate people unto God: untainted, pure, and holy.

Everyone on earth needs an authority, higher power, someone superior to them, an entity that is greater than themselves, who can bring sense and sensibility to life on this earth. We seek to have a purpose with our lives that is bigger than ourselves.

When we forsake what God has told us through the Bible, Jesus's life, and the Holy Spirit speaking to our hearts in agreement with the Bible and Jesus's life, we too go astray from God's plan and purpose for our lives.

When we lose our connection with the authority and communication from God, we develop our concept of God. As we develop our concept of God, we create him to be just exactly what we want him to be. It is not based on any authority from God. We call this a designer god. We each then have a god personally designed for us—our individual god.

In this concept everyone does what is right in their eyes because God is only seen through their eyes.

If this bothers you and you ask how this can be, go back and read the book of Judges, and it becomes quite clear that even today this is a problem in our world.

Why would anybody want to try to create, or should I say recreate, God to be something other than he is? There are many reasons. None of them are valid. In chapter 30 we will cover this in great depth.

For now, we need to understand that this Levite left the principles taught in the Torah and leaned upon his knowledge, and this began the designer god movement. In chapter 30 we will discuss not only the reasons people do this but also look at the progressive history up to modern time.

CHAPTER 21

"There Is No God" Suitor

Psalm 14:1

"The fool hath said in his heart, there is no God."

This fifth and final suitor to God is the most unlikely one. This is the suitor that says, "I will ignore the whole issue of God. I will pretend he's not real. I'll say he doesn't exist." Some in this group will say I don't know if there's a God therefore I will ignore him.

How then can they be a suitor to God? There is an old expression that says, "Ignorance is no excuse for breaking the law." There is enough evidence to show that God exists. There is not enough evidence to prove that God exists to those who do not want to accept the evidence already given. Some people just will not admit the evidence is true.

I worked as a paramedic in Oregon for over twenty-five years. I worked on the streets of small towns and large cities. I estimate that I cared for over twenty thousand patients. No, I did not see it all, but I saw enough to feel confident in making this statement. People will believe in what they want to believe in and will deny what they don't want to admit.

I could recount many calls that had this same scenario. An ambulance is called because somebody's having chest pain or shortness of breath or pain in their back or pain in their left shoulder and arm or even a toothache. They wanted me as a paramedic to help them get rid of the pain and take it away. Upon my evaluation of the patient's condition, I would share with them that the evidence of their EKG and physical exam tells me they are having a heart attack. Invariably, the patient would say no, I can't be having a heart attack because I have too much to do or I'm too young or I just don't believe you know what you're talking about.

While we are having this discussion and I am trying to convince them to let me treat them and transport them to a hospital quickly in order to save their life and they are telling me they're not going to go because they will get over it, they go into cardiac arrest and either die because we can't resuscitate him or we resuscitate and then beat feet to the hospital.

I saw this over and over. One evening, I stood in the reception area at the University of Oregon Health Science Center emergency room. A man walked in with his right hand cusped behind his neck. He explained to the receptionist that he was in an automobile accident two nights before and his neck has hurt ever since. In the course of checking in he stated the ambulance people wanted to take him to the hospital, but he didn't think it was bad enough.

When the receptionist asked if this had become worse since the accident he said, "Not really, but when I turned my head sideways my neck feels different." He tried forcing his head sideways to demonstrate the problem and completed a fracture of the first two vertebrae in his neck. It completely paralyzed him and stopped his breathing. The man died in the ER that night.

I could tell you story after story of people ignoring the facts and having a catastrophic end either to their life or for the rest of their life. I choose to tell you this only to help you see that the atheist, agnostic, scientific doubter, or the person who chooses just to ignore the facts about God is no different than all these people.

They simply program themselves to ignore the issue of God. Jesus understood this when he said that if his disciples did not worship him the stones on the ground would call out his praise. All mankind groans from within their deeper being to know God intimately.

Some of the patients mentioned above had a little different twist but with the same outcome. They would say, okay, maybe I am having that heart attack, but I am busy right now; or I'm not convinced it's as bad as you say. Some will say that they are sure that they will be okay if they just rest and maybe see their doctor in a day or two if it gets worse. Too often we would be forced to leave the home and the patient behind due to the patient's refusal. Later that same day the patient would go into cardiac arrest and die.

One group of patients said they did not believe they were having a heart attack and refused to acknowledge the truth and died. The other group of patients would acknowledge the possibilities but invariably chose to deal with them in their way ignoring the facts the paramedic discovers, only to end in cardiac arrest.

I find then this parallels a spiritual truth. There are two basic kinds of people when it comes to God. There are those who say they don't believe in God; and there are those who say God may be real, but I believe that whatever I am God will accept it, and I will be okay when I die because I didn't do anything so terrible against him.

There are those who deny allowing their spirit to speak and use only their mind, and there are those who listen to their spirit and subject their mind to it.

Let me explain this. Those who rely only on their brain make comments like this, "I only believe the facts, or it has to be scientifically proven." They have a hard time believing in their emotional/spiritual self.

There are those who rely only on their spiritual guide. They make comments like, "I feel, it feels like, my heart tells me, or I need to meditate before I can tell you the answer." They have a hard time making decisions based on logic and need a spiritual guide.

There actually is a third group in a sense. There are those who combine both using wisdom and intuition or reasoning and spiritual sense to guide them.

The reason I say they fall into two categories is because both that second and third group can believe in God and can have a relationship with him. Those who rely on scientific evidence lack the very ingredient mandatory to believe in God. That is they cannot rely on faith.

God knew that man would have difficulty trying to prove that God exists. In fact, God has planned matters so that we could not prove his existence any more than we can prove his nonexistence. It is because God wants us to relate to him with faith. In fact, without faith it is impossible to please him. Our entire relationship with God is built and sustained through the power of faith. We must have faith that he is and faith in our relationship with him.

It is this group of doubters, unbelievers, and unconvinced who have trouble with any relationship when faith is involved. You will find these people have difficulty with trust. Trust comes from faith.

This group I call the unlikely suitor because they seek to find God by physical proof only. They demand tangible evidence. Because they demand evidence of God in order to believe in him they are simply saying, I am angry because he doesn't reveal himself to me in the way I want him to, therefore, I'm going to say there is no God. The answer is the fool has said in his heart there is no God. This unlikely suitor will still fight to be right and in the end when God judges them for not believing they will stand indignantly and say, but you did not prove you were real to me how could you expect me to believe.

CHAPTER **22**

Struggles with Identity

1 Corinthians 3:3

*"For you are yet carnal: for whereas there is
among you envying, and strife, and divisions,
are you not carnal, and walk as men?"*

Over the next five or six hundred years, the *church* took a turn for the worse. Though Christianity had grown and flourished throughout all of Europe and the Middle East there seemed to be something amiss. The church, which was primarily the Catholic church, dominated Christian beliefs.

The love letters were scattered about the world in different people's hands. Many of them were in the hands of the Catholic church. They were locked away where only the leaders of the church could read them. The only way they could be copied was by hand and even that would need translating from language to language. It wasn't until the fifteenth century when Tyndale rendered the first translation into English. In the late 1400s the Gutenberg press was invented but not available for mass production for some time.

Miracles as performed by the apostles had died out; they (miracles) were few and far between. It was the intent of the church to share the gospel with the entire world and thereby have all of the people in the world become Christians. Unfortunately, the techniques employed to accomplish this were counter productive.

Church hierarchy became corrupt and powerful and deeply involved with coercion of the leaders, to preach only that which was sanctioned by the church. When scholars and clergy disagreed with the church there would be an inquisition followed by an edict to recant. In the process, men of God were tortured unto death if they did not recant.

Great men such as Wycliffe, Tyndale, Luther, and John Huss were all persecuted or killed, enduring great torture because they spoke out against the Catholic church doctrine.

There were no less than seven crusades from the western Christian group to try to unite with the eastern Christian group, all of which were unsuccessful in the end. The Crusades were fraught with corruption even though the initial intent was to rebuild harmony. In one crusade the children were sent out, thinking because they were pure they could not be harmed. Those that were not killed were sold into slavery.

Then there were the wars with the Muslims who had settled into Spain and southern Europe and were driven out because the Christians were stronger.

Is it any wonder they called it the dark ages? The common person had to trust the diocese of the Catholic church who was extremely corrupt.

There is one thing that attributes to the way people acted from the second or third century until the present time. It is common to Christians. It is the dependency on a few to interpret the Scripture. Then it was never put into a complete work. That left theology and Christianity on its own. The emphasis was placed on reading the Scripture and carrying out to the letter of the law that which they thought the Scripture conveyed. If you look at the history of this time period, you will see that people had simply to do what the spiritual leaders told them. There was no importance placed on a spiritual, emotional, and personal relationship with God. It was an impersonal, duty-bound obedience to do what the Scripture said.

While the Holy Spirit had been given to all mankind, there was none or little teaching regarding a relationship with God. In fact, what was taught was that people had to go through a priest in order to even have a relationship with God. Absolution (salvation) was achieved by confessing to a priest and receiving the sacraments.

It wasn't until Martin Luther nailed his thesis on the door of the cathedral, which stated that anyone could approach God without going through a priest that began to change minds about having a personal relationship with God. That was the fifteenth century.

Is it any wonder that Christianity was so brutal and bloody through this time? No one relied on a personal direction from God. The Holy Spirit was not called upon to guide people into the truth. The matter of the heart was not even a concern. When truth is only a matter of mental assent and reason without grace to temper we resort to our own abilities.

Having done this, the people lacked for compassion in serving Christ.

Let's put all of this in terms of courtship between Jesus and his church (the bride). When Jesus went away to prepare a place for us, he gave two things as we said in previous chapters: the Holy Spirit and his love letters.

The love letters were kept and read by his people who perused the letters over and over. But without talking directly with Jesus they were left to read the letters and decide for themselves the meaning. Just like a normal relationship between a man and a woman. If the man went off to war and left only a handful of letters behind, over a period of time it is highly likely that the woman would eventually make more of each word than what was originally intended.

The church changed hands generation after generation and the understanding of the letters seem to be changed according to the generation who is interpreting them. One may make the argument that the Holy Spirit guided them in their interpretation. I can only say that when you look at the years of growth and corruption in the church, coupled with the emphasis on performance and no emphasis on relationship, it leaves me to believe that the leadership of the Holy Spirit was not a premium in people's hearts and minds.

I belabor this point only to this regard, we will see in the next few chapters how important the interpretation of the Scripture and the leadership of the Holy Spirit in the church are to the maturing of the bride. All relationships thrive on direct communication in each other's presence. That is true for the church and God, a man and a woman, and Jesus and his bride-to-be.

Chapter 23

The Great Awakenings

Psalm 119:105

"Thy word is a lamp unto my feet, and a light unto my path."

2 Timothy 2:15

"Study to show thyself approved unto God,
a workman that needeth not to be ashamed,
rightly dividing the word of truth."

2 Corinthians 3:6

"Who also has made us able ministers of the New
Testament; not of the letter, but of the Spirit: for
the letter killeth, but the spirit giveth life."

"Be not conformed to this world: but be you transformed
by the renewing of your mind, that you may prove what
is the good, acceptable, and perfect, will of God."
(Romans 12:2)

From the early to mid-1500s, the influence of men such as Martin Luther and John Calvin began to influence the church. They presented opposition to the Catholic church in the basic theology of salvation, baptism in water, and living a life that was different from Catholicism. They influenced men such as Jacobus Arminius, John Knox, and Menno Simons. They and others in the late fifteenth century strongly rebelled against the Church of England.

This led to the development of groups of people in various Protestant and Catholic churches to form a purer religion. These people were given the name of Puritans. The Puritans called for the Church of England to return to a purer form of religion similar to that of the early church in the time of Christ. Of course this raised great concerns for the Church of England. In 1604 the Puritans met with King James of England and asked that the church recognize the Puritan way. They went away disappointed, and as we all know in 1620, they sailed the Mayflower to America.

Not only did the Puritans come to America, but other people seeking religious freedom came to America. Christians spread out with their new thoughts from England throughout Europe and into America.

Out of this dissatisfying meeting came the edict of King James, *that a translation be made of the whole Bible, as consistent as can be to the original Hebrew and Greek; and this to be finished and printed, without any marginal notes, and only to be used in all churches of England in times of divine service.* Forty-seven men from Westminster, Cambridge, and Oxford universities work to put together what we know is a King James Bible the completed form was issued in 1611. While the authorized version has undergone revisions, the latest of which was 1638 became printed by 1632.

With the advantage of being able to print on the Gutenberg press the written Bible and pieces of Bible writings were more readily available. By the mid-1700s the King James Bible was well known throughout the civilized world. Other translations such as the Geneva Bible and Tyndale version became less relied upon.

From the beginning of this explosion, the call by Christians and other groups to study the Bible and begin to rigidly follow its teachings, until the late 1800s, was the theme of Christian growth. Many new churches and doctrinal variations sprang up during this time. This was a time of developing deep theologies and finding new themes in the Bible.

This newly discovered information caused a tremendous revival and awakening of the church. This was also the beginning of the awakening of the study of people and how they responded to the gospel. So much so that the father of psychology, Carl Jung, said that all psychology was a study in the journey for man to meet himself and to meet deity.

This was a time of new discoveries. People were discovering new insights in the Bible. They were discovering new insights to God. People were discovering new insights to themselves. It was a great time of experimentation. All this led to the beginning of discoveries in all aspects of life.

America had just been discovered and a wide-open land was available for people to explore and discover. With the land came discoveries of new element deposits. This brought discoveries of new uses for the elements. It was a time of great freedom and challenge.

The church was no exception. The discoveries in the Bible, and the freedom to find land where colonies could be established, led to practice and experiment in their newfound religious beliefs. It was a time of developing many churches which became organizations and, consequently, founded many of America's early colleges.

From all of these church groups, from those who held to Catholicism to those who radically developed a small sect of believers, from Puritans to Presbyterians, there was a core of people who were serious about their relationship with God. They lived it to the fullest of their abilities. They attempted to refine and live every jot and tittles of the Bible, according to their understanding. This wonderful Bible, from Genesis to Revelation as put together by King James, became the foundation of their lives, faith, and relationship to God.

These were men and women of faith. They believed God. Jesus was there Savior. They grew, became strong, and banded together and fought for their beliefs. While these Americans split hairs about doctrine they stood together on their belief in Jesus as their Savior. They believed enough alike to understand that they needed to build one country, under God, and centered on Christ. They realized that to allow other countries such as England, Spain, and France to control any part of their country, or any piece of their society would be a recanting of their faith and a loss of their freedom.

Consequently, America became the United States of America, one nation, *under God*, with liberty and justice for all. They formed the constitution, a government controlled by a Senate and House of Representatives, and a management branch. They also formed a judicial branch known as the court system. The Supreme Court building was built with Moses and the Ten Commandments etched above their entry door and also above their ruling bench. This was to signify the strength of our country's faith in Judeo Christianity.

In chapter 15 we introduced the love letters from Jesus to his beloved, the one he fell in love with. We watched how the church, like a woman, finishes school and is ready to start life. She meets her prince, falls in love, and then he is taken away to prepare a place for them to live happily ever after.

She takes the love letters to her secret chambers and ponders them over and over, taking into her heart all the wonderful things he has said. During that time she grew as an individual sharing her excitement with others. We saw in chapters 16-21 that others claimed that the prince loved them and not her. There were the great arguments (wars of the dark ages) with no one gaining the upper hand, and all getting stronger in their beliefs about their each being the chosen one.

Now we see this bride-to-be maturing into a self-confident, knowledgeable, and strong woman. In reading her love letters, over and over, she gains insights and begins to put the picture together about her true love. She now sees a new side of him and devotes herself to loving him, pleasing him, and doing all things just the way he said he would like them done.

She takes on this task undaunted, with great zeal and excitement, and a determination to prepare for his return.

Unfortunately, it is a time when she lives within her knowledge of the letters. She lives within the letter of the law, perfecting every behavior she possesses and action she pursues. All of this is wonderful and produces growth and yet something seems to be missing. All this time she is missing the one she does all of this for Jesus. Surely, her heart has grown lonely for the one she adores.

You might ask, where is the Holy Spirit in all of this to give her comfort? As we look at the history of the church from the establishment of the Catholic church to the mid-1800s, there is little if any mention about the work of the Holy Spirit. Writings about the church, the Bible, or the relationship between God and man focuses on carrying out the intent of the Bible and the interpretation of the Bible.

I believe it to be natural that the bride, being left with the letters as tangible evidence of her beloved, focuses on doing what it says and allowing her relationship to be held to the feelings of her heart for spiritual connection.

If we did not have the Bible to teach us about the Holy Spirit we may not even understand his existence or participation in our lives. It is a natural pursuit to learn something, investigate it, and then pursue.

All of this speaks to the buildup of knowledge and wisdom by the bride-to-be whom we call Christians. It is the setup for the next step in the relationship. It is the last step of preparing the Christians for Jesus to come and claim his bride.

CHAPTER 24

The Last Days:
The Eighth Dispensation

James 5:7-8

*"Be patient therefore, brethren, unto the coming of the
Lord. Behold, the husbandman waited for the precious
fruit of the earth, and have long patience for it, until he
received the early and latter rain. Be also patient; establish
your hearts: for the coming of the Lord draw nigh."*

We have looked at the seven dispensations so far. They are the Edenic, Adamic, Noahic, Abrahamic, Mosaic, Davidic, and the New or Grace dispensations. Now we want to look at the eighth dispensation: the last days. In each of these dispensations we have seen how each one parallels a growth phase of that of a human from birth to mature adulthood. We even see how adulthood has several phases of its own.

Now we are going to spend a few chapters looking at that part of adulthood, which covers the final chapter before being married. Like a man and woman who have romanced each other and have spent time getting to know thoroughly, and have completely adapted to each other, become engaged to be married. The engagement period is a special time of preparation for the wedding. It is a time of becoming completely committed and living in that commitment as a final step of preparation.

This time, like no other, develops the deeper knowledge of each other, enters a deep spiritual, emotional, and intellectual intimacy that bonds them so strongly that it carries them into that marriage relationship that lasts for life. All the things that marriage provides, short of the physical consummation, are provided during this engagement. It is this time period that affirms the couple's belief that their marriage will endure through life.

If this time of engagement falls short of equal confirmation of their love to one another the marriage will fail or fall short of God's intended purpose for it.

All of this is what occurs between God and his people (Jesus and his bride) in the last days. Simply put, the last days are a special time when God prepares his people for the coming of his son to claim his bride.

We call this time "the Last Days" because the climax or end of this time, as signified by the coming of Christ in the clouds of glory.

Like other dispensations it has a beginning, a covenant, and an end. This fits the criteria for dispensation.

Since this book is dedicated to helping us understand that we live in the last days, we will cover this time period over many chapters.

I was raised in the Assemblies of God church. My father was one of the best Bible teachers I have sat under. In Bible college I sat under the teaching of Ralph Riggs. He was one of the original founders of the Assembly of God church. He was a great Bible teacher. I revered him not only as a teacher but as a true man of God; a man of grace and wisdom. Both he and my father shared their beliefs in the seven dispensations. They lumped the former and latter rain and the last days all into the dispensation of grace. This is known as the Church Age.

This doctrine is based on the understanding that when Jesus died, was resurrected, and ascended to heaven, and then the Holy Spirit was poured out on the day of Pentecost, the Church Age began. This Church Age would end with the resurrection of saints. There is a variety of views regarding whether the resurrection will take place before the tribulation—during the tribulation or after the tribulation. That I suppose would make the Church Age overlapping into the time of the apocalypse as described in the book of Revelations.

You may say at this point, "What difference does it make?"

The difference has a deep theological impact.

If the Church Age was all one age then while many signs and events would point to the coming of Christ, there would be no change in the way we relate to Christ. The doctrines of salvation, water baptism, fruits of the Spirit, and how the church functions, would have no collective progression. In other words, the same salvation experience that was experienced by Christians in the early church—believers in the third century, sixth century, fifteenth century, eighteenth century, and even in the twenty-first century—would never be any different and would have the same doctrinal base. This doctrine, if followed, says that we will have individual growth in God, but there is no collective growth in the church.

I present to you in this book that we see through the Bible a collective maturing of humans in their relationship with God. Some people have been a part of that collective group called the Bride while others have not. Those who have not have formed many different ideologies about how they want God to work but deny the path that says Jesus is the only way.

The bride of Christ, the Elect one, is a collective group that has grown like a human being has grown. And in the last days we see the completeness, the maturity, the fullness of the stature of Christ; in this bride we call the church.

There are many people who have formed strong pseudo-Christian groups based on collective salvation. They do not believe in the individual salvation through Jesus and his atonement for our sin. There are those also who believe only in individual salvation. Many born-again Christians have adopted this belief, some without understanding they have adopted it.

Some people feel that salvation is personal and comes about by confessing your sins and asking Jesus to forgive and cleanse them. They grow in Christ, fellowship with a church, do all they feel God asked of them, and believe that is the extent of being a Christian.

It is my feeling that we cannot just become a part of a belief system—trusting that system, be it a church or a secular religious group—and inherit eternal life through it. It is also my feeling that a Christian who has experienced Christ's forgiveness and lives the life he calls them to can disassociate with the collective bride of Christ in these the last days.

If we adopt the belief that salvation is purely individual and not collective we have missed the whole point of the Bible.

> *Revelations 19:7-9 let us be glad and rejoice, and give honor to Him: for the marriage of the Lamb is come, and His wife hath made herself ready. And to her was granted that she should be arrayed in fine linen, clean and white: for the fine linen is the righteousness of the saints. And He saith unto me, write, blessed are they which are called to the marriage supper of the Lamb.*

In this Scripture we see the bride is a collective of the saints but spoken of as though it were an individual.

At this point you may be ready to throw this book down and scream, "Heresy!" You may even feel so strong as to throw it in the fireplace. I am not expecting you to agree with me at this point. I have given you a very subjective idea.

The chapters to come will be more objective, and I challenge you to hang on until the end. The evidence of what I share about the last days is overwhelming, both external and internal.

CHAPTER 25

The Last Days: External and Internal Evidence

Luke 21:25

"And there shall be signs in the sun, and in the moon, and the stars; and upon the earth distress of nations, with perplexity; the sea and the waves roaring."

1 Peter 2:9

"But you are a chosen generation, a Royal priesthood, a holy nation, a peculiar people; that you should show forth the praises of him who hath called you out of darkness into his marvelous light."

There are two types of evidence regarding God's work in the last days. These are external and internal evidence. Evidence, as used for this purpose, comes in many forms. All evidence discussed in the next few chapters, pertaining to the last days, is biblically based with Scripture references. All quotes are from King James Bible.

External Evidence

External evidence, of the last days, is that which is prophesied in the Scripture and happens outside or separate from the body of Christ. This includes the seemingly natural phenomenon which happens to the planet, the solar system, and man-made structures. It also includes things that occur with people but not associated with the relationship between God and his bride, unless the association occurs between the Bride and other people. External evidence almost always has a negative component to it.

In terms of the last days, external evidence is not connected directly with God's judgment on man as it is seen in the book of Revelation. It is connected with God's judgment on this earth because of Adam and Eve's sin. God cursed the ground because of Adam and Eve's sin.

> *Genesis 3:17 ". . . and unto Adam He said, because thou hast hearkened unto the voice of thy wife, and hast eaten of the tree, of which I commanded thee, saying, thou shalt not eat of it, cursed is the ground for thy sake; in sorrow shalt thou eat of it all the days of thy life.*

Sometimes people get confused about what God does, how he does it, and why he does it.

We must remember God created a perfect world with a perfect Eden. He created man and woman because he wanted to have their companionship. He loves them. Had they not sinned, they would still be living there today. It is because of their sin that things have gone downhill ever since. It is the natural progression of degeneration from that point until the time of the great apocalypse.

Over the period of 6,000+ years the earth has slowly eroded and is becoming more volatile. It is the result of natural degradation of elements and microorganisms.

God's intent is always for good. Satan's intent is always for bad. Neither God nor Satan makes earthquakes or volcanoes. They are a natural result of God's curse on the earth for sin. This earth deterioration will slowly continue.

The same is true of people. Adam and Eve had perfect bodies. God designed them to live eternally. Due to their sin God told them that the process of dying and death would happen to everyone. Mankind lived hundreds of years before death ensued. Over a period of hundreds and hundreds of years, the natural result of living on an imperfect planet resulted in physical degeneration and illness, injury, and death.

I hear many Christians say that God tests us by giving us bad things or troubles in our lives so that we will be better Christians. I hope to debunk this ungodly notion and that you will be set free from such an oppressive belief. The Jews looked at ailing and deformed bodies which had imperfections as being a direct result of sin.

> *John 9:2-4 "And his disciples asked Him, saying, Master, who did sin, this man, or his parents, that he was born blind? Jesus answered, neither hath this man sinned, nor his parents: but that the works of God should*

be made manifest in him. I must work the works of Him
that sent me, while it is day; the night comes, when no
man can work."

Jesus comment was that nobody sinned. But he was sent to heal the blind man. The blindness was a result of millenniums of degradation of the human body.

Then you might say, "So if God didn't design us to be sick, why doesn't he just heal everybody and make them well?"

The answer may not be what you want to hear. The consequence of the original sin is the deterioration of man and his environment. It is a natural law placed into effect by man's sin. This body and this mind are subject to flaws, frailty, and death as a consequence of sin. It is collective and progressive and not necessarily personal. God does not interfere with the natural laws because if he did it would nullify the consequence of our right to choose. As long as mankind is sinful the consequence of aging will be present.

I never cease to be amazed that parents resist the temptation many times to rescue their little children from the consequences of their misbehavior. In fact they understand very clearly the necessity of children learning that bad behavior has bad consequences and suffering the consequences helps us to learn: to perform better behavior. Yet as adults, the same people expect God to nullify any consequence of our rebellion or misbehavior. We expect God to take away all the bad no matter how much we ignore his rules or his fellowship.

The good news is that in spite of Adam and Eve's sin, and the consequence of aging and death, he has made a way that if we recognize we are part of that consequence and turn our life to him through Jesus. He will restore eternal life: not on this earth but in the life to come. Otherwise, we will suffer with Adam the consequence of sin because we are rejecting God's plan just as Adam did in the garden. That consequence is eternal death

One final note in this regard is the progressiveness of the deterioration. In other words, the longer mankind lives the more signs of illnesses and degenerating bodies and minds will be evident.

The same goes for the earth and the cosmos. The change and deterioration of the earth that was created perfect has slowly increased and will till the end of time. It will increase to the point of total destruction.

> *Revelation 21:1, "And I saw a new heaven and a new earth: for the first heaven and the first earth were passed away."*

Internal Evidence

Internal evidence is that evidence which relates to the events pertaining to this bride of Christ. From the time of Adam and Eve, God has always had a people whom he communicated with and were a part of the bride. Internal evidence is the documentation of facts pertaining to this people.

Internal evidence contains logistical, historical, physical, and spiritual facts. The facts may be documented by those within the bride or from sources outside the bride. We focus much of our attention on prophecies in the Bible concerning God's dealings with his people.

When prophecy occurs in the Bible, Christians believe it and unbelievers scoff at it. When prophecy is fulfilled as described in the Bible, it becomes fact. Today's Christians accept most of and unbelievers scoff at it. The controversy of prophecy in the New

Testament pertaining to the apocalypse is a good example of believers who disagree on the interpretation.

Since the death of the apostles people have differed in their interpretation of the meaning of the New Testament writings. The more those writings became more available, the more diverse the interpretations became. In the time of the great awakening people became scholars of the Bible. As we stated in that chapter, they dissected every jot and tittle. In the last days, this is even more evident.

One thing has remained common with internal evidence up until now. We use our brains increasingly to understand the Bible. We, at the same time, have not found a new revelation in the most important area of internal evidence. That area is in what is God doing in the world today.

The area of internal evidence that is the most important of all is that of the revelation of the church's purpose in the last days. People use their knowledge and wisdom to decide the church's purpose yet have not come to the recognition of the most important part in the church's history.

The internal evidence I'm talking about is the evidence that we develop in our spirit. It is the personal relationship with Jesus that goes beyond our understanding. It is that relationship of the heart where God speaks with us in intimacy.

When I need time alone with my savior, I take myself to a place like the garden of Gethsemane. I meet with him there and we talk. There I can share my deepest of feelings for him, needs, and concerns. While basking in his presence, I can share my appreciation to him. It is in these times that I learned the value of being in his presence always. What I learn and gain from this meeting in the garden guides me through all the other time when I can't be there. It is my truth, my rock, and my life. Perhaps you identify with this as well.

This relationship is the evidence that Jesus is alive. It is greater than my mind can comprehend from reading that Jesus died for me. It is more powerful to guide my life than anything or everything I have learned and comprehend with my mind. It is more powerful than any other relationship or concept that I know. It is *the* greatest evidence of Jesus and what life is about that exists.

In the days of the great awakening, the church had an awakening intellectually, which turned their minds and attentions to God. Their hearts were made full by their knowledge and understanding of new revelations of his word to them.

In the last days there is another great awakening. It is the final awakening. It is the church becoming awake to the spiritual relationship with God and applying knowledge gained by a personal relationship, where the Holy Spirit gives the interpretation and direction. This brings life. The knowledge of the Bible without it is death. This is recognized by the vibrancy, joy, and sense of anticipation being heightened increasingly as the Lords return nears.

> *2 Corinthians 3:6, "Who also hath made us able ministers of the New Testament; not of the letter, but of the Spirit: for the letter killeth, but the spirit giveth life."*

CHAPTER 26

The Last Days: Knowledge Shall Be Increased

Matthew 24:33

"So likewise ye, when ye shall see all these things, know that it is near, even at the doors."

Daniel 12:4

"But thou, O Daniel, shut up the words, and seal the book, even to the time of the end: many shall run to and fro and knowledge shall be increased.

When we look at the prophetical phenomenon spoken of in the Bible, we must be aware that there are three distinct times to which it refers. The first is the time from the beginning until the last days. The second is the time in which we refer to as last days. The third is the apocalyptic times, which occur after the last days. Our focus will be on the last days. I will only refer to the other time periods at times and then only to show a contrast or to validate your belief in the last days.

I realize there are different opinions on prophecies in the Bible, both in the Old and New Testaments, and about when the fulfillment of that prophecy should occur, or whether there is more than one time frame for the prophecy. I will let you be the judge.

In the Scripture quoted above God told Daniel three very important pieces of things to come. First, he tells Daniel to shut up the books until the time of the end. Second, he tells Daniel that people will run to and fro seeking information. Third, he tells Daniel that knowledge will be increased at that time.

When God told Daniel to shut up the books, he was telling Daniel that the revelation of the information he gave Daniel would not be understood until the end times. God closed the door of understanding for the man. However, it also means that at the in time of last days that the understanding would be revealed.

God showed Daniel great things about the end times and yet this one Scripture is quite overlooked. The time of the end is the same time that Paul writes about in 2 Timothy 3:1-8, where Paul says that in those last days people will be ever learning but never able to understand the truth. While knowledge is increased in the last days, the understanding of why it is increasing and the purpose of the knowledge will elude people. Mankind will thirst for and find knowledge but miss the whole point, having a form of Godliness but denying the power thereof.

Both of these refer to the last days before Jesus comes. Simply put, there will be a great increase in knowledge and people seeking knowledge but not able to understand the truth of what they learn.

Our first benchmark to understanding the last days is to realize that the increase in knowledge is not just the everyday, average we're-a-little-bit-smarter type increase. It must be a profound and measurable increase.

When Adam and Eve left the garden they had the crudest of tools to work with. God told Adam he would till the ground by the sweat of his brow. This was new to Adam. He was not a farmer he was just taken care of by God in a garden. Everything grew and he ate what he wanted and never worried about more growing. Now he had to work.

He told Eve that her childbearing would have pain. And that eventually they would both die. This meant the process of death would not be without debilitation and deterioration of the body over time.

They had no idea what this meant and no way to deal with it. Over the next five thousand eight hundred years they made progress one step at a time toward understanding and developing tools and methods to deal with their issues. This growth was slow. During the five thousand eight hundred years they went from walking on foot to riding horses or being pulled in carts by animals. Their farm tools remained quite crude and involved horses pulling plows and harrows to till the land.

Medicine was slowly discovered in plant material and over generations and generations they refined slowly some understanding of the healing arts. If we look at the progress made in the sciences it was a slow progress with very minimal advances in automation.

The mechanical sciences had little advancements. They learned about many metals but the abilities to work the metals were limited to a fire pit forge to melt, shape, and harden them.

It's from 1800 to the present time that knowledge in every science and art has exponentially increased. In other words, in the first fifty-eight centuries of man's history knowledge doubled maybe once every hundred years, but in the last two centuries it started doubling much more rapidly. That knowledge in the 1800s doubled in fifty years; by 1900, it doubled every twenty years; by 1960, it doubled every ten years; and today, it doubles in two to five years.

Mankind walked then rode a horse then used the cart, and by the 1800s developed a steam engine that could be used to transport people in a vehicle. Harnessing steam as a power source took about one thousand eight hundred years to develop. Then the next hundred years the internal combustion engine was developed. Over the next sixty years, rocket engines were developed that could propel people into space.

Through the centuries man developed crude weapons such as clubs, spears, and then bows with arrows. Eventually explosives were discovered and developed into a form of rocketry. Eventually gun powder was used in crude weapons to propel projectiles out a barrel and became known as a gun or rifle. In the 1700s guns were loaded with powder, a projectile (usually a ball of lead or iron), and using a fuse or cap, were fired from a pistol, rifle, or canon. By 1900 gunpowder and weapons were refined to the point of capability of firing multiple rounds per minute and distances greater than a mile. They used shells with casings and bullets instead of muzzle loading.

By 1945 mankind developed the ability to destroy with a bomb that could kill eighty thousand people in a single shot. Today, a mere sixty years later, we have weapons that use technology, which can kill living beings for one thousand yards in every direction from the point of impact and not destroy a house or any structure around. We have technology and weaponry that can trace a projectile to pinpoint target miles away and penetrate a cemented bunker and blow up that cemented building.

We rode horses, then cars, then spaceships, and airplanes. The Wright brothers historically flew their airplane in the air for several hundred feet and marked the beginning of flight. I am alive and writing this book and able to tell you about my grandmother, whom I spent many days listening to share her life. She told me about her helping to cook lunch and dinner at that historic flight for the Wright brothers. On December 17, 1903, there were four flights, the last one went 852 feet, at an altitude of 500 feet, and lasted just fifty-nine seconds.

In the short time from that historic flight until today we have been able to develop an unmanned airplane that can fly over twenty-four hours at a time, thousands of feet in the air, and fire a rocket from so far away that he could not be seen by the naked eye of the person it pinpoints as a target and hit that selected target dead on.

In medicine, through trial and error, people discovered plants and materials that could help them get better or make them worse. They also discovered things they could do to help them feel better. This was the extent of medicine for centuries. Again, it took centuries and centuries to unlock the mysteries of the body and its functions.

The first concept of a microscope was invented by a piece of glass that was sphere shaped in approximately AD 1000. By 1590 Zacharias and Hans Jansen developed the forerunner for the compound microscope and telescope. The electron microscope wasn't invented until 1931 by Ernst Ruska. This was a major breakthrough in how to view cells of the body.

It has only been in the last forty years that we have discovered that we can identify people by their DNA. We can now take magnetic resonance imaging pictures and see bone structure as clear as if it were skinned back and held in front of our eyes. We can swallow a pill and as it goes through our digestive system it will send information back to a computer explaining what is wrong with us. We swap hearts, lungs, kidneys, and many other parts as commonly as we exchange greetings with one another. In every avenue of medicine there have been tremendous discoveries in just the last five to ten years.

Twelve years ago I had an aldosteronoma removed that was undetectable by even a CT scan. Ten years prior, I would have died without it even being detected had it not been for modern medicine.

New diseases are being discovered all the time. In fact, in the last hundred years diseases that never existed are not only being discovered but are becoming deadly to masses of people. With these diseases the new technologies available to study them and the knowledge of how to treat them is being discovered as well. This is all escalating in the last hundred years and continues to escalate exponentially as we count the years.

Less than two hundred fifty years ago, Paul Revere rode a horse through the countryside announcing that the British were coming. The Revolutionary war occurred and its chief source of communication between the military leaders of each side and their respective countries and supporters, was for a courier to carry written letters between them. Word-of-mouth from the battlefield to the people back home, either America or England was the only way they found out what was happening. It could take months to hear the outcome of the battle and plan the next strategy.

Recently we witnessed uprisings in the Middle East countries like Egypt, Yemen, and Syria. The news about what was happening was live within seconds of its happening due to the vast amount of people with cell phones, iPhones, and iPads. Media such as Facebook and Twitter allowed people to share with hundreds of thousands of others around the world exactly what was happening. They not only could tell people what was happening but were able to take pictures and transmit them via satellite around the world. This technology was not available fifty years ago.

People of my age can remember the days before there was television, computers, jets, satellites, laser beams, or Super Bowls. Electronic technology is growing faster and faster every day. It is almost like I buy an electronic handheld device in the morning and go home to try it out, only to see on my computer that there is a new model available.

The understanding of our own minds has rapidly grown in the last century. For five thousand eight hundred years, man has slowly grown to understand behaviors, interactions between people, and studied how people think in order to either find peace and compatibility or figure out how to defeat their enemy. And in the last hundred years, much energy has been devoted by people beginning with Sigmund Freud and Carl Jung to the study of the mind. Today, the world is prolific with professionals called psychologists and psychiatrists, whose life is dedicated to the study of the mind.

There are also the medical doctors who team up with the psychological doctors to study the brain. These people actually study the chemical and neurological structures and interactions in the physical brain. All of this information they gather has exponentially increased our understanding of people and how they think, behave, and process information. It is only in the last forty years that they have even attempted and successfully completed brain surgeries with skills that allow them to remove pieces of brain and leave people still functional.

Indeed, every area of life has its own technology. And if we look at the increased knowledge in any area of our lives we will see a common denominator over history. There is a slow and gradual increase in knowledge from 4000 BC to about AD 1000, then take curve slightly increasing information from AD 1000 to AD 1800 and then a sweeping increasingly steep upswing from 1800 to the present day. This upward arcing curve will continue until the day Jesus returns and takes his bride to heaven.

It is not just the technology world that has increased in knowledge and had an explosion in their knowledge in these last days. The church has increased in knowledge. I shared in previous chapters how the printing press and the printing of the King James Bible has spread the gospel around the world and helped everybody to understand the Bible better by having their own personal Bible study. I want to emphasize this point. The Bible as we understand it to be all sixty-six books of the King James Bible has only existed in the hands of people for about four hundred years. With the coming of increased communications, ability to move about the world rapidly and begin ever increasing access ability to books and ideologies through other media; knowledge of the Bible has increased rapidly among those who study it.

Since about 1900 the church has spread around the world. The technologies that we have just discussed have facilitated access to more interpretations of the Bible, more translations of the Bible, and more books and writings about each small individual piece of the Bible. This has increased the church's knowledge base for interpreting the Bible. This has grown at an accelerated pace in the last hundred years like everything else.

There have been more translations and versions of the Bible written in the last one hundred years then there were in the rest of man's history. It is a testimony to the pouring out of knowledge on God's church. The clarification of each word in the Bible according to its original language has become not only a passion but an obsessive quest by many. The hunger of the church to better define the message of the Bible is an unquenchable thirst. This sounds good and truly we should hunger to know the Lord better.

Books, DVDs, and CDs about the Bible and Christian living are being produced en mass every day. There is no end to available information about any subject in the Bible.

This thirst for information began slowly in the fifteenth century and slowly gained momentum into the eighteenth century. By the 1900s the pace quickened from a walk to a run. Today the church, as well as other religions, is in a mad dash to the finish. They are reaching out for anything they can get their hands on to shore up their faith and refine their position in the mad race to find God.

While some are finding truth and growing in their relationship with God, through salvation by Jesus, and leadership of the Holy Spirit, the vast majority of people who seek God fall into that category referred to by Daniel and Paul. They run to and fro seeking truth but are unable to understand it when they see it. They find that chief cornerstone, the rock of offense, and turn away looking for something, they know not what.

This is a sign of the end time. It is not a sign because it's happening, but rather, it's a sign because of the mass quantity and intensity of the people caught up in seeking answers and never finding solutions.

If we look at this picture we can only say that we are surely in that time Daniel spoke of, ever learning but unable to come to the knowledge of truth.

CHAPTER 27

The Last Days: Wars and Rumors of Wars

Mark 13:6-13

"For many shall come in my name, saying, I am Christ; and shall deceive many and when you shall hear of wars and rumors of wars, be not troubled: for such things must needs be; but the end shall not be yet for nation shall rise against nation, and kingdom against kingdom: and there shall be earthquakes in divers places, there shall be famines and trouble: These are the beginning of sorrows. Take heed to yourselves: for they shall deliver you up to councils; and in the synagogues you will be beaten: and you shall be brought before rulers and kings for my sake, for a testimony against them. And the gospel must first be published among all nations. But when they shall lead you, and deliver you up, take no thought beforehand what you shall speak, neither do you premeditated: but whatsoever shall be given you in that hour, that speak you: for it is not you that speak, but the Holy Ghost. Brother shall betray brother to the death, and the father the son; and children shall rise up against their parents, and shall cause them to be put to death and you shall be hated of all men for my namesake: but he that shall endure unto the end, the same shall be saved."

Religious Connection to the Wars

Once again, we must ask ourselves, what distinguishes wars and rumors of wars in the last days from all other times? Since Jesus spoke these words quoted from Mark 13, there have been wars going on throughout the known world continuously. At times many countries were involved, in other times maybe only one or two countries would be involved. How do we know the difference between a surge in wars that involves several nations and the last days surge in wars?

People tend to look at the surge in wars and rumors of wars at a given moment and compare that moment in time with what's gone on in their lives previously. Some people just look at all the wars that are going on at the moment, become overwhelmed, and say this is surely what Jesus was talking about.

Take a look at Mark 13, Matthew 24, and Luke 21, who all record Jesus's words on the subject. Jesus puts things in a chronological order so that we might understand the difference between what has gone on for thousands of years, what will happen in the last days, and what will happen during the tribulation. He cites some specifics about the last days in these chapters.

In Mark 13:5, Jesus starts out by saying that let nobody deceive you. There are a lot of deceptive ideas and beliefs that crop up every time another war starts, or the threat of war, which is bigger than we can cope with in our minds. When fifteen countries it in the Middle East and Northern Africa have a simultaneous revolution and it is tagged the Arab Spring, our reactions are to run to the Scripture and find one that supports the idea that this is connected within the times.

Just because it's a different kind of war and it includes many countries that threaten our country's existence does not mean that it is the last day's war. There must be something more in connection with it.

Make no mistake I believe this Arab Spring is very much a part of the last days: not because it's big or threatening, but because there is some deeper things connected with it and altogether these events address last days issues. The next five chapters I will discuss all of these other issues.

What we must be careful to do is to look at what the last days are about and then look at the current events and how they pertain to the Scripture. When we link Jesus words to be aware of the events of the last days and not be deceived by people simply pointing and saying, "See what's happening it's the last days."

The next thing Jesus makes clear is that many will link wars and rumors of wars to people standing up and saying I will save you. Jesus said many would proclaim at this time: "I am Christ." The proclamation that one is Christ in time to save the world from the destruction of wars must be distinguished from those who are antichrists. Antichrist's are associated with a destructive power and fight against God and good.

My father, who lived through World War II, said that many Christians believed Hitler was the antichrist referred to in Revelation and other Scriptures. In the fifties, sixties, and seventies, I heard many people get tagged as the antichrist. Stalin, Ayatollah Khomeini, President John Kennedy, and many others had Christians questioning, "Are they the one?" But never was it said of any of those accused of possibly being the antichrist, that they were the savior, come to save the world.

The ones who come saying they can solve the world's problems and will save us from destruction are the false christs. These people have existed since Jesus's time. The apostle Paul and the apostle

Peter and the apostle John all warned of these people. Jesus wanted us to understand that in the last days there would be great threats to Christians as well as persecution and that would be accompanied by people saying they will save us. That combination occurs in the last days.

In other words, the same people who claim to have answers and are there to fix the world are also those people who are going to persecute the Christians and turn their backs on the Israelis. Can you see that happening in our world today?

The last day's wars as well as the apocalyptic wars are connected to the values connected with God. That is what sets them apart from wars in the past. Now before you get too excited and say, many, many wars have been fought in the past connected with religion: this is just one of many factors that come together to indicate the last days.

Nation against Nation

In World War II, the Great War, nearly every nation in the world became involved. Many thought it would lead to the Armageddon. At the termination of World War II, alliances, such as NATO, SEATO, OPEC, and the communist bloc, were created to protect the interest of multiple countries with similar interests. The introduction of nuclear weapons posed great threats to people around the world. As I shared at the beginning of this book, many Christians believe that Jesus would come any day and looked at the wars that have ensued and the constant rumors of wars that plagued the world.

The rise of powerful nations and diverse ideologies have only served to proliferate the fear and angst between nations. Nations have increasingly formed alliances with like-minded nations to either protect themselves or to help them further their own cause.

The latest demonstration of this is the uprising and revolution seen in the Middle East countries who are all in an alliance of Muslim ideology and focused on the destruction of Israel.

While the tension between nations and the wars and threats of wars between nations have always existed, the steady and constant increase in threats and skirmishes between nations has grown to the point that virtually no country on earth today can say they are immune to threat, revolution, or invasion by another country. If there is a relationship between current events and Mark 13:8, it is just this: the scope of worldwide instability and constant turmoil globally between nations. The tension is mounting, and one of these days we will see the great explosion.

Kingdoms Will War against Kingdoms

It is no wonder that Jesus said in the same sentence that nations would rise against nations and kingdoms would rise against kingdoms. They go hand in hand. Just as there have always been wars between countries, there have always been wars between kingdoms. The intensity of kingdoms and kings wanting to establish a larger powerbase continues to propel kingdoms into war.

We must note the difference between a kingdom and a nation. A nation comprises a land mass with physical boundaries and specific social, economic, and, more importantly, legal systems. A kingdom comprises an ideology, be it religious, political, or other driving force that has no specific boundaries or claims to being a named country.

There are two basic kingdoms in this world. They are the kingdom of God and the kingdom of Satan. Kingdoms begin with one and spread to another and another. The kingdom can be very small consisting of two people, or it may be very large, consisting of millions.

A person can actually isolate themselves: declare themselves king of their own presence and rule over only a small place and a few animals. A man with the shack and a dog living alone in the woods is the king of his domain.

When the children of Israel settled in Canaan, they sought for a king. They chose Saul to be the king for he was head and shoulders above all others. Saul was an elected king. He ruled over a group of people who had one God, who were joined together both by family and by faith in the writings of Moses.

Queen Elizabeth of the United Kingdom inherited her kingdom by virtue of family right. She has little to do with the judiciary running of her country. Her primary role is to solidify the country as a figurehead of principles her countrymen possess. While having many functions and duties related to the country, such as détente with other countries, there are no elections and her reign is in the hearts of her people.

Jesus is the king of the church (the bride).

> *1 Timothy 1:17, "Now unto the King eternal, immortal, invisible, the only wise God, be honor glory for ever and ever."*

Here Paul extols Jesus as the eternal king above all. He never had a country, his crown was made of thorns, he was never adorned with gold and jewelry, and yet to this day, two thousand years later, he has ruled over the hearts of more people than any other king who ever lived.

You and I have a kingdom. Each of us is a king over those whom God gives us. Please note that in the spiritual sense, king is nongender.

> *Revelation 1:5, "Jesus Christ, who is the faithful witness, and the first begotten of the dead, and the prince of the kings of the earth. Unto Him that loved us, and washed us from our sins in His own blood, and has made us kings and priests unto God and His father; to Him be glory and dominion for ever and ever. Behold, He cometh with clouds; and every eye shall see Him and they also which pierced Him: and all kindreds of the earth shall wail because of Him."*

For those of us who know Jesus as king of their hearts and lives, he has appointed us to be rulers over our lives and advocates for Jesus, who influence others to make Jesus their king as well.

We can only rule over our own personal life. However, each of us will influence many people by our lives. It is how we represent our king, Jesus, and how we present him to others that determine the kind of kingdom we reign over.

I will address this more in the upcoming chapters.

> *Matthew 4:8-9, "Again, the devil taketh Him up into an exceeding high mountain, and showed Him all the kingdoms of the world, and the glory of them; and said to Him, all these things will I give thee, if thou wilt fall down and worship me."*

Every person who ever lived on this earth since Adam and Eve has a kingdom. Some of us have a kingdom of one and some of us have kingdoms of millions of people. When Satan showed Jesus the kingdoms of the world, he clearly was showing Jesus the people who had not made Jesus their king. His kingdom was vast numerically. In this verse it is clear that those who do not make Jesus their king have made Satan their king. Satan offered to Jesus all of the kingdoms of the world. He could only offer that which he had.

Many people rejecting Christ would not confess they serve Satan. I believe that nobody on the face of this earth would serve Satan if they truly knew him for what he is: a liar and a thief, who has come to steal every man's soul from God. I also believe every person wants to be accepted in the presence of God and approved by him.

The problem begins when a person decides to rule their kingdom their way and without making Jesus the King of their lives. Every person has an opportunity to choose to make God their king or not. Those who choose not to let God be the king of their lives, by default, choose Satan.

Since Adam and Eve believed the lie of Satan and chose to build their kingdom without God's blueprint for their life there has been two groups of people on the earth. Those that accept God's kingdom authority and those who do not. With the dispersion of mankind after the Tower of Babel, many ideas of what God wanted and how he wanted to build his kingdom in them were developed. This was because they did not have direct communication from God.

From the time of Abraham and Isaac, God has spoken to his bride first through his relationship with the Israelites and finally through his relationship with those who accept Christ as savior.

Jesus said, "I am the truth." Everybody, from the time of their birth is confronted with truth. The truth leads us to God. As some grow up they develop doubts about various truths. Doubt comes from Satan. Satan is a liar whose intent is to lie and cast doubt and confusion about the truth. This is the basis of all conflicts. If everybody believed the truth that God chose them there would be no conflict on earth.

If everybody believed the truth (God, Jesus, Holy Spirit), God would lead them into a relationship of faith in him.

Satan is not the lord of a single lie, Satan tells many lies. Thus he leads many people astray, in different directions, which causes confusion among those who do not believe in Jesus.

It is so important for us to understand the building of the kingdoms of God and of Satan because it is the basis of all wars.

Those who believe in God and give their lives to him are kings in God's kingdom. Those who do not believe in God are kings in Satan's kingdom. We all are kings over our kingdom.

Because nobody has all the truth and some seem to have no truth at all we will always have difference of opinion. Some differences people accept and live with. Some people feel they are so right that they must fix the differences in other people. They may try to fix others' differences through reasoning together or go to the other extreme and tell others you see things my way, or I will kill you. And finally there are those who seek to destroy others with a different opinion through subtle means, such as, verbal abuse, discrediting people in public or to others around them, in enacting laws to force their way upon others, or in listing others of like mind to shun the friendship of those who disagree with them.

This kingdom building is the basis of wars. The kingdom wars referred to in our base Scripture for this chapter start with an individual and their kingdom. When they can impress, convince, or even force another to believe their way, their kingdom expands.

One by one the kingdoms grow. Little kingdoms develop into bigger kingdoms with smaller kingdoms becoming a part of the bigger kingdom. Ten kingdoms of one become one kingdom of ten and so on and so forth.

In the last days, Jesus said, kingdoms will war against kingdoms. The days in which we now live are the last days and the wars we see and hear about are wars of kingdoms. The many kingdoms of Satan war against each other and have for millenniums. However, in these last days their focus will increasingly turn to the destruction of Christians and Jews.

The many kingdoms of God have for centuries made war against each other. This is natural and represents the internal conflicts of the bride. But as the last days are upon us, and the coming of the Lord approaches when he shall claim his bride, those internal conflicts will cease and be resolved and the wars of the kingdom of God will focus on not wrestling with people but with principalities and powers. In these last days, we not only should focus on fighting the wiles of Satan but we will, as a bride, also focus on fighting the evil and not trying to fix our brother and sister in the Lord.

> *Ephesians 6:12, "For we wrestle not against flesh and blood but against principalities, against powers, against the rulers of darkness of this world, against spiritual wickedness in high places."*

While this Scripture has always been true, we must recognize that it has never been truer than in the last days. Turning our wars toward spiritual warfare is not just praying against the powers of Satan. In these last days we must recognize that our warfare must be the breaking down of strongholds of Satan in the kingdoms of those who belong to him. Breaking down these kingdoms means wrestling or grappling with the powerful hold the lies and untruths that Satan has convinced people to believe.

Principalities are the kingdoms. The powers are the powers of lies told by Satan. The truth is mightier than the sword. This war is not about winning the world for Jesus. Someday he will rein mightily over all people. This war is about preparing ourselves to be a bride of kingdoms for God. It's about setting our house in order and making it a lighthouse in a dark world. It's about Jesus coming for *us* and our preparation for his coming.

CHAPTER 28

The Last Days: Perilous Times

2 Timothy 3:1-6

"This know also, that in the last days perilous times shall come. For men shall be lovers of their own selves, covetous, boasters, proud, blasphemers, disobedient to parents, unthankful, unholy, without natural affection, truce breakers, false accusers, incontinent, fierce, despisers of those that are good, traitors, heady, high-minded, lovers of pleasures more than lovers of God; having a form of godliness, but denying the power thereof: from such turn away. For of this sort are they which creep into houses and leads silly women laden with sins, led away with divers lusts."

Lovers of Self

Since the time when Abel's sacrifice pleased God and Cain was jealous, and henceforth slew his brother, there have been perilous times. There are always times when people are in perilous times. So what makes the last days perilous times different from other times?

Scripture notes three major things that cause perils in the last days. First, there is a major absorption in self. Second, there is little tolerance for those who do not accept the self-absorption and evil involved. Third, there is a violent and rampant pursuit of power over others and destruction of those who get in the way.

Let's just look at some of the many ways that human selfishness has become tantamount in the world.

Some might say that people have always been somewhat self-focused, and self-centered. Never before in the history of mankind has it been so widespread throughout the world and so commonly accepted among individuals on the face of the earth.

One common phrase that I hear quite often, quoted in all sincerity, is "You have to take care of yourself first before you can take care of others." Nothing could be farther from the truth. Tell it to Jesus. He gave up his life that we might live. He teaches us to lay down our lives for him. This is just one of the ways in which people concoct ideas that sounds so good and right, but are so wrong, evil, and selfish. No wonder the Bible says "the heart of man is deceitfully wicked, who can know it?"

Let me paraphrase 2 Timothy 3:2, "People shall become so consumed with themselves, their lives, what they are about, comparing themselves to others, who they are and what they have that they cannot even consider other people's needs wants or desires. They see other people with something that they don't have or they would like and begin to lust and want that for themselves so they can be equal or better than others. They then boast of what they have and who they are. It then becomes more important for people to recognize them being better than others. They see the recognition and puff out their chest with pride, looking at what they have accomplished. Then looking at others, tear them down to make them less than themselves. They become eventually unthankful, ungrateful, and separated from God's way.'

Disobedience to Parents

For thousands of years children have been under parental rule. No matter what society we look, the general population supported the belief that children were under the rule of their parents. If children misbehaved, they were given to their parents for correction. Christian societies, especially the United States, followed the Apostle Paul's words for children to obey their *parents*.

It has only been in the last fifty or sixty years that a change has occurred, and step-by-step, has developed a society where children are not even under parental rule but seemingly on loan by the state to pay for and watch over them: abiding by the state's governing rules.

I say this because I first started with the definition of child abuse. When I was a kid and misbehaved, I could look forward to a paddling on my backside. Today that is considered abusive and if somebody were to see that occur, they reported to the police, and the next thing you know, the child is in a foster home.

Our children learn early through modern media and educational formats that their rights are over parental rights. When in history have you read of children suing or taking to court their parents over a rights issue? But it has occurred and is increasing in America.

Without Natural Affection

There has also been a breakdown of the home and the family unit in America and other countries. Divorce rate is at an all-time high, disparagement from marriage and family raising has become quite in vogue, and homosexuality is becoming a tremendous issue.

The concept of a father and mother with children living in a house, where father goes to work and mother tends and children go off to school in the morning and then they all come back together in the evening as a family unit is becoming more unique and rare every day. The support and appreciation for this lifestyle that has been an accepted way of life for millenniums is now considered an alternative way of living.

I hear comments such as "children who are raised in homes with one parent have just as good an outcome as children who have a mother and father together in their home." Today statistics do not bear that out. This is not to say it cannot be done, and in some cases done well. However, it is not the norm.

Isn't it interesting that when psychologists began teaching against discipline of the children, and saying those children's problems were products of parents, that from that point on we began to have increasing crime rates, increasing homosexuality, and increasing divorce rates.

The loss of the natural affections husbands have for their wives, wives for their husbands, parents toward their children, children toward their parents, and the love and appreciation for their relatives and extended families is a way of life supported and promoted in our society today. It is sad but it is prophesied in the Scripture above. When a father cannot hug his daughter and say I love you without someone thinking incest is a good indication that the mindset of our society has fallen to a deep low.

Our schools, our courts and our teachings are increasingly upholding the deviation from the natural affection of male and female. Not only are our children being taught to accept those who are trapped in the evil web of homosexuality, they are being taught, and courts are supporting, that homosexuality is an acceptable and even at times preferable way of life. Never in the history of man has it been as intensely promoted as it is today.

I believe all of this speaks to the fact that when we break away from that which God intended in natural affections destructive behavior begins. Those affections that are appropriate and natural between a husband and wife, parent and child, siblings, and friendships, build healthy, happy, long-lasting and productive relationships.

In the last days the evidence of the breakdown in natural affections is seen in gross abundance through the proliferation of children turning against parents, and parents losing even the right to control their children, is directly related to crime and homosexual proliferation in America.

One scripture that points this out is found in the book of Mark.

> *Mark 13:12-13, "Now the brother shall betray brother to death and the father the son; and children shall rise up against their parents, and shall cause them to be put to death. And you shall be hated of all men for my namesake but he that shall endure the end, the same shall be saved."*

Tolerance for Evil

Not only is there a tremendous proliferation of ungodly behavior in the last days there is pressure for tolerance by those who perform the ungodly behavior. Darkness loves darkness. The children of darkness demand tolerance for their darkness because the light spread by the children of light shows them for who they are.

> *1 Thessalonians 5:4-6, "But ye, are not in darkness, that that day should overtake you as a thief. Ye are all the children of light, and the children of the day: we are not of the night, nor of darkness. Therefore let us not sleep, as do others; but let us watch and be sober"*

One of the earmarks of the last days is the depth of the darkness and the intensity of the demand for tolerance of the darkness. I will address this more in the next few chapters.

Increasing Violent Behavior

Finally, because of resistance in the last days to the children of light, children of darkness will resort to more and more violence. This violent demeanor leads up to the wars of the last days.

Can you see the tension mounting around you? Look at the increased tension in your life. Our political arena over the last fifty years has become more and more aggressive and violent. Each time a new party gains control of the White House, Senate, or House of Representatives, the incoming party works harder to reverse the effects of the opposite party preceding. It doesn't seem to matter whether it is Democrat or Republican; they just wage a more intense war strategically to gain their will. They struggle to control the courts by placing politically oriented judges in power instead of judges given only to doing the right thing. They remove great military leaders and replace them with military leaders of political agreement.

Each time there is a change in political leadership in our country, the intensity increases, and the stress, frustration, anger, and violent behavior is increased.

There are people in high places with a tremendous amount of wealth, influence, and power upon the leaders of all facets in our country and around the globe. These people have in mind to destroy our sense of democracy based on Judeo-Christian beliefs. They wish to usher in a new world order based on darkness, tolerance for all evil things, and suppression all those who oppose them.

These are the earmarks of the last days. There are many more that we will cover in future chapters. The intensity of all that I shared in this chapter is of such magnitude that it could only be accomplished in the last days. It reaches to all kingdoms on the entire globe. No person will be left unaffected by what is coming in this near future.

These are perilous times. These are the times we live in today, when no one feels safe and everyone feels threatened. Our values based on Christ and the Bible is being pursued for destruction with unparalleled historical intensity and ferocity.

It is building up to a war of kingdoms against kingdoms, father against son, neighbor against neighbor, and people against people. It is not a war of countries against countries but rather faith against faith. It is not a war of Republicans against Democrats as the Tea Party clearly indicates. It is a war of ideologies, powers, and will against will.

Make no mistake about it, never before has a global warfare affected people against people. It is well understood by our government and military that our war on terrorism transcends borders of countries. The war of radical Islam and others want to control the world. They do not even recognize borders of countries. *This is the last days!* Can this lead to the great tribulation, Armageddon, and the destruction of this earth? How soon is this going to occur? Can we intervene and postpone these last days or must we realize it is about over and Jesus is preparing to return and take us off of this earth?

We cannot sleep any longer. For us to think at this time, that somehow our illustrious and most powerful government is going to solve our problems and save our lives and land and preserve our country and traditions is putting our heads in the sand as an ostrich and expecting it to all be better when we pull it back out.

CHAPTER 29

The Last Days: "There Is No God" Suitor

Luke 12:19-21

"And I will say to my soul, soul, thou hast much goods laid up for many years; take thine ease, eat, drink, and be merry. But God said unto him, thou fool, this night thy soul shall be required of thee: then whose shall those things be, which now has provided? So is he that lay up treasure for himself, and is not rich toward God."

Psalm 53:1

"The fool hath said in his heart, there is no God."

If there is a God, why is there so much death, destruction, and suffering going on in the world? This is the lament for the unbeliever. They cannot reconcile the evil of the world with an all-knowing, all-powerful, kind, and loving God.

Every person, in the deepest secret chamber of their heart, cries out to God. It is when they cannot connect with him that they turn away from the true way of finding him and seek him through their own means.

As I said in an earlier chapter, instead of following their heart with faith they resort to finding him intellectually through fact and tangible science. It is impossible to prove God through science. God designed it that way. Without faith it is impossible to please God, or to even know him.

So what then is to become of the unbeliever? The wisest man to ever live addresses this issue in the book of Ecclesiastes. Simply put, he said that for the unbeliever everything is vanity—in vain. His conclusion was to fear God and keep his commandments.

If a person does not believe in God they have no hope of a life after death. Therefore all that they have lived for is themselves and what they have in life here on earth. There is no point in doing good, helping others, or even loving beyond doing that which gives them some gain on this earth.

Is it any wonder then that their values are selfish and self-serving.

In this discussion there are only two groups of people: those who love God keep his commandments and those who do not believe and lift themselves.

While the unbeliever says in their heart there is no God, they must recognize that to serve themselves or any other purpose or entity is to be serving Satan. Satan is the god of this world. He is the lord of darkness. God is the Lord of light. There is no God of the gray zone. There is no gray zone.

With no hope of afterlife one's only reward is to fulfill their pleasure upon this earth. Their pleasures for a season, instead of investing in eternal rewards, are referred to in Hebrews.

What is the path of those who choose sin for a season?

The first thing a person, lacking in faith, does is to resort to an intellectual argument of science proving what is true or not true. It is turning to the mind and intellectualism instead of increasing faith.

This sets up an odd paradox. The more they seek intellectually to prove God's existence or nonexistence the farther into darkness and away from God they get. The farther into darkness they get the more convinced they are that God does not exist; and they then demand more proof that God exists. This frustration serves only to cause anger and resentment toward those who walk in the light.

The next step is to become hostile toward those in the light because they have peace, joy, and a purpose for living which extends beyond the grave.

This hostility turns to violence and the unbeliever seeks the destruction then of the believers. This has led to war, mass slaughter and destruction of Christians and Jews who have the light.

This is exemplified in the lives of such people as Attila the Hun, Hitler, Stalin, Lenin, and many other fierce conquerors.

So now you say: I get it. What does this have to do with the last days?

I explained the process of death and mass destruction by darkness against light so that we might understand that process which has gone on for years is present today. Not only is it present today but is intensified many times over.

The wars that we talked about in previous chapters are not wars over political ideology. They are not even wars over land and countries. These are wars between darkness and light.

It is imperative that we as believers, members of the bride of Christ, understand that darkness waging war against light is what this world is all about. Since Cain slew Abel it has been darkness trying to destroy the light.

When the bride entered that time of puberty so to speak, in the time of Abraham, chapter 11, the bride-to-be became aware of other suitors. Darkness hating light became more apparent with Ishmael, the wild child, and Isaac the son of blessing. As we talked, in chapters 15-19, about the other groups who became suitors for God's blessing we saw how the seeds of hatred and violence grew from individuals into groups of individuals led by angry and godless men.

As the last days approach and now are present, these suitors have grown into polarized, large, and powerful entities. They struggle to dominate with the power of darkness over the bride. They recognize more clearly every day the righteousness of the true bride and God's approval of her. Therefore their intensity to destroy the bride increases.

True authority comes from God and is given to those who walk with him. Because darkness and Satan have no authority from God they exert power to mock him and his people.

> *Matthew 11:12, "From the days of John the Baptist until now the kingdom of heaven suffereth violence and the violent take it by force."*

Here, Jesus explains this principle. John the Baptist preached the truth and it shed light on Herod and Herodias's sin. Herod placed

John in prison and later ordered John to be beheaded. Jesus now explains the principle of how violent people in darkness will treat those who shed light on sin. He wasn't just talking about John, appointed to the principle that will apply until the end of time. That principle has intensified until this day and will continue to intensify on exponential increase until Jesus returns.

> *Matthew 24:14, "The gospel of the kingdom shall be preached in all the world for a witness unto all nations; and then the end shall come."*

Many people will say this type of violence has always been present and therefore isn't a mark of the last days. Jesus said that in the last days the effects of the gospel being preached would be to every nation in the world. I have listened to some folks argue: that means only to the nations that were known in the days of those who lived when the Bible was written. Certainly the known nations of the world in AD 100 did not cover the entire earth. A mark of the end days then meant that the last days could not occur until the earth was populated and the gospel was given to everybody in every country.

We have reached that benchmark in the last century. I remember as a child in the 1950s hearing reports from missionaries that they had spoken to tribes in South America who had never seen a white person and never heard the gospel. Now the nations have all heard the gospel.

It is the time when the unbelievers, atheist, agnostics, and others are preparing an all-out assault on the kingdom of God. This means that by whatever means possible, they will persecute with the intent of eradicating from the face of the earth any light and every awareness of God and Christians. They do this because they are so angered at the light that God shines on their sins through Christians that they, like Herod, order the death of Christianity and Christians.

Many people like George Soros, Madeleine Murray, and Charles Darwin, are avowed to atheism and all the evil that goes with it and wishes only to take down all Christian countries and Israel. They work methodically, wielding their power through money and influence and other resources to destroy all knowledge and faith in God and usher in a godless one world government. They are joined by millions of people around the world who deny that God exists.

Right now as you read this, in America, there is a surge by a movement to neutralize and destroy all Christian influence. The atheistic believers in socialism have launched an all-out war to destroy the democracy of America, western Europe, and Israel. The only thing that stands in their way is the Christians and Jews. Throughout history in the entire world, democracy has only come at the hands of the Christians and Jews.

Remove the Christians and Jews and this world becomes a playground of the evil and corrupt. If you look at all of the interest groups that are supported by the atheistic, socialist one soon learns that the picture the apostle Paul paints, in Romans 1, is exactly what is coming about today.

The orchestration of the Arab Spring, the Occupy Wall Street protesters, the demands of people around the world for all rich people to give their money to the people who do not work, the influx of illegal aliens in America being embraced by the U.S. administration, and the empowerment of China is all orchestrated at tearing down America. Their attacks are withheld only by the Christian people in this country and Israel.

We must understand that we are in a spiritual battle. Those who are on Satan's side are doing everything possible to destroy

Christians. They are going about this methodically, covertly, through the legal system, intimidation and through violence.

This group is organized and viciously advancing worldwide. They are spending vast sums of money and great amounts of energy to accomplish their agenda.

We must recognize that in all of their denial their true heart's desire is calling for God to reveal himself. That day will come when Jesus will reveal himself. But because they cannot believe without proof there is no hope for them to come to know Jesus as their savior until they choose to have faith that Jesus is and is the son of God.

While they deny God's existence, their goal is to prove they are right and it is the only way to live. They will challenge God to show himself. God will show himself in that great and notable day of judgment.

CHAPTER 30

The Last Days: The People with the Designer God

Matthew 7:23

"They are workers of lawlessness."

2 Peter 3:3

"There shall come in the Last Days scoffers walking after their own lusts."

2 Peter 2:17-19

"They are wells without water, they speak great swelling words of vanity to allure through the lusts of the flesh, and promise liberty while they themselves are the servants of corruption."

"The designer god" people are an eclectic group. We learned in a previous chapter about this culture and that it started with the Tower of Babel. In the dispersing of the people around the world, not only their language was changed, over the centuries their relationship with God changed. They were left to go their own way and made up rules and lore about God.

Virtually, every culture has contributed to this group: those who were Christians and Jews, as well as other cultures, have chosen to ignore or defy the truth of how we are to relate to God.

Romans 1:21-32 explains the process as to how these people went from the Tower of Babel and unity to the present time, the last days. Here shows a picture of the steps of progression from knowing God, to not honoring him as God, to becoming unthankful, and to relying on their concepts of God.

This changed their perception of God, from a pure and glory-filled God to a humanized God after their concepts of what they wanted him to be.

From this they continuously changed their images of God from truth to whatever they needed or wanted for their convenience.

With this continual change of truth about God everyone in this group have their own God according to their design. As one person put it to me, "Everybody has their own path to God."

As we learn from Genesis and the story of Noah, we know that when mankind is left to their imaginations they become wicked in every way. So the paths of the "designer god" people have each found their wicked way in these last days.

While there are as many concepts of God as there are people in this group there are some common threads within them. Does any of these quotes ring true with you? "I do right by people so God will do right by me," "If God wants me he knows where to find me," "I believe in God, I just don't believe in the Bible." "If God is as loving as the Bible says he is then I'm okay."

You see, they have decided what God accepts and doesn't accept. They don't accept the Bible because they don't want to live by its standard.

In the last days, as described in the Bible, these people will take on a specific persona. It is described in many places, but 2 Peter 3 is one of the better illustrations. It paints this picture of a person who wants to do and be what they create themselves to be. They not only ask everybody to accept them for who they are but to accept their relationship with God as equal and is as right as everybody else's relationship with God. They may think Jesus was a good person but that he is not the son of God. They may think they are okay and that the need of a savior is just plain ludicrous. Yet they will ask the Christian to accept their path to God as being equally valid as those who believe in Jesus's birth, death, resurrection, and shed blood for our salvation.

In short they deny that Jesus is the only way to the Father and insist that everybody has their own way to heaven. While they demand equality they are willing to render only that equality to everyone who agrees with them. They will accept the Christian as having their way to heaven: but that way through Jesus is just another way. I've had people from this group get angry at me because I would not admit that I believe in just another way like them.

What marks this group as a significant sign of the last days? If they have been around and developing for centuries, what makes them different today? You probably have already asked these questions.

In the last days the growth, by sheer numbers and percent of population of people around the world who feel so strongly about this theological philosophy has become so great that they have now become a movement. They are to themselves a religion of sorts to be reckoned with. Groups such as those who believe in "the secret," or God is just energy of all people, where God is made up of all people, but deny the Bible and the truth, have become a collective of ideology. They are becoming a united force with a venomous agenda specifically toward the Christians. They are united as a front with atheist and politically divergent groups to eradicate Christians and Jews from the face of the earth.

The other thing that is a sign of the last days in regards to this group, is their anger and frustration with Christians in this that we hold a standard of morals that impugn their life style. The Bible explains God's views on how life should be lived among people. There are moral standards of behavior that he has set in place without variance or repentance.

The acceptance of the moral code that says you can have your lifestyle as long as it doesn't hurt me personally, and I can have mine as long as it doesn't hurt you personally, allows that any behavior is acceptable as long as you don't infringe on another's space.

Look closely what it says in Romans 1:24-28.

"Therefore God also gave them up to uncleanliness through the lust of their own hearts, to dishonor their own bodies between themselves: who changed the truth of God into a lie, and worshiped and served the creature more than the Creator, who is blessed forever, Amen.

For this cause God gave them up to vile affections: for even their women did change the natural use into that which is against nature: and likewise also the men leaving the natural use of the woman, burned in their lust one toward another; men with men working that which is unseemly, and receiving in themselves that recompense of their error which was meet. And even as they did not like to retain God in their knowledge, God gave them over to a reprobate mind, to do those things which are not appropriate. The film without unrighteousness fornication, wickedness, covetousness, maliciousness; full of envy, murder, debate, deceit, malignity, whisperers, that biters, haters of God, despite, proud, posters, inventors of evil things, disobedient to parents, without understanding, covenant breakers, without natural affection, implacable, unmerciful: who knowing the judgment of God, that they which commit such things are worthy of death, not only do the same, but have pleasure in them that do them."

Let's understand this clearly. There is a chain of wrong decisions by those people who do not want to recognize God for who he is. People start with the opportunity to make a choice for good. When they make a bad choice and they begin to harden their hearts against God, even being unthankful for his patience in all he has done for them, they turn to themselves for wisdom. God has no other choice than to let them be and do as they wish.

God will not ever force his will upon us but will always honor our choices. God does not want anyone to perish but will respect the choices of people to destroy themselves.

In the last days this, group of rebellious, people turn to their own wicked imaginations and do all kinds of evil. To clearly understand what is wicked and evil, we must look at the history of Satan with mankind to determine their definitions. The Bible refers to Satan as the evil one. He is evil because of his original sin. That sin was doing what he wanted instead of what God wanted. *It seems his basic premise was: I don't hate God, I just don't want to be ruled by him.* His statement to Eve in the garden was not one of overt hatred or rebellion against God. His argument was that she could be like God with increased knowledge.

The evil, of everything, is simply defined as anything that is not acceptable to God. To understand what is and what isn't acceptable to God, we must understand him through the interpretation of the Bible first and then rely upon the Holy Spirit to guide us into truth. The Bible and the Holy Spirit never disagree. Why, you might ask? It is because the Bible is God's love letter and the Holy Spirit is one of the Godhead. One is written, the other oral. Both are from God.

When Satan was in heaven with God and knew God, he did not honor God as God. This is his evil. When we on this earth who have the opportunity to know God but honoring him not as God, we become evil. Evil does not exist in us because we do terrible things. Whatever we do is either evil or good based on the reason we do it.

This is why some people who are really good people and would never harm anybody, are gentle and kind and practice honesty with all intent of doing good, are still not considered acceptable by God. Because their intent is about themselves and what they think is right. They do not honor God. They do not seek his will and bow to his authority. They live a life that leads to destruction. What more can one say than to love God and keep his commandments. Remember, to keep his commandments means to accept what he writes to us to do and what he speaks to us to do.

Now when you read this dissertation in Romans you can see the progression into a downward path of self-exultation, by people who do not honor God. In the last days it isn't enough for these people just to be a good person and live and let live. The last days are marked by this group wanting no reminder that they need God or even that there is a God of the Bible. They worship what they have created more than the creator. In a very real and practical way they worship themselves, the creature, more than the real creator.

The days of Noah and the days of Lot are called out in Luke by Jesus as "last days" signs when this group satiates in self pleasure and self-indulgence.

Luke 17:26-30

As it was in the days of Noah, so shall it be also in the days of the Son of Man. They did eat, they drink, they married wives, they were given in marriage, until the day that Noah entered into the ark, and the flood came and destroyed them all. Likewise also as it was in the days of Lot; they did it, they drink, they bought, they sold, they planted, they build; but the same day that Lot went out of Sodom it rained fire and brimstone from heaven, and destroyed them all.

In the days of Noah people who had become so thoroughly and intractably evil (turned away from God) that he decided to destroy all except Noah and his family.

Genesis 5:5-7

"And God saw that the wickedness of man was great in the earth, and that every imagination of the thoughts of his heart was only evil continually. And it repented the Lord that he had made man on the earth, and it grieved him at his heart. And the Lord said, I will destroy man whom I have created from the face of the earth; both man, and beast."

There is a common word in Genesis and Romans that explains why this is the last days and why God is going to destroy these people and this earth in the end. That word is *imagination*. In both cases man turned from God's way to their way and did what they imagined was right as opposed to what God said was right. Imagination is defined as creating an image or picture from one's own conceived thinking. This leads everyone to believe and do whatever they can picture in their mind.

God is not the author nor the originator of bad things. He wants only good and gives only good to the world. It is in the last days that God says if you really want the evil then I will let you have your reprobate mind demands and not stand in your way. There is a time of reckoning coming at the end of the last days. However, God will not interfere with plans will and therefore we see the evil described in Romans.

I interject at this point: *this is why we have a written set of love letters from God.* It is so that we all can read and understand the truth alike. Unfortunately, those who aren't in love cannot appreciate nor understand what is written in love letters intended only for the one who loves the writer.

Examples of what people imagine to do without God are scattered throughout the Bible. Romans, Galatians, Ephesians, first and second Peter are some of the places you'll find lists of such things.

In Luke, God singles something thing specifically as an earmark of evil in the last days. Jesus says that it will be like in the days of Lot. If you recall the story of Lot it was about the rampant obsession with homosexuality in the cities of Sodom and Gomorrah.

In the last days, homosexuality becomes viewed differently by those who create their god from their imaginations. This pervasive practice was so prevalent in Sodom and Gomorrah that God destroyed the cities. Through the centuries this practice has sprung up in different cultures and different times. However, it has always been an unacceptable behavior in Godly societies. Renounced by God in Deuteronomy and punished later when practiced by the Israelites in times of King Asa and Jehoshaphat, this unnatural relationship between same-sex is considered evil by God at all times.

Today it is amazing how societies respond to this behavior. It is renounced by the Christian and Muslim religions. But today the polytheistic and ungodly people not only embrace this behavior but are demanding acceptance and appreciation for it among the Christians.

In America laws have been passed to protect the rights and to endorse their behavior. Schools are being required to teach the practice as not only acceptable but as desirable as well. While these laws are being flown under the guise of freedom for a minority group, under the flag of equal rights, Christians who want to share their belief are being shut up because of separation of church and state.

Isn't it amazing that Christians could not share their beliefs because they are coming from God, but homosexuals can share their beliefs because they are rejecting God and his word.

Not only does the homosexual movement want to be free from anything or anybody that is not joining in celebrating their evil they also want to destroy and be rid of anyone or anything that reminds them of their wrongdoing.

The gay-rights movement seems to be another sect of *the many paths to God* and *there is no God* groups.

I mentioned in the first chapter that another earmark of the last days is that group will be more militant and violent toward the Christians. They not only want their way, and not God's way, they also don't want any reminder of God because it makes them feel bad knowing that they are in rebellion to him.

CHAPTER 31

The Last Days: Islam— The Holy Warriors

Galatians 4:27-5:1

"Now we brethren, as Isaac was, are the children of promise. But as then he that was born after the flesh persecuted him that was born after the Spirit, even so it is now. Never the less, what saith the scripture? Cast out the bond-woman and her son: for the son of the bondwoman shall not be heir with the son of the freewoman. So then, brethren, we are not the children of the bondwoman, but of the free. Stand fast therefore in the liberty wherewith Christ has made us free, and be not entangled again with the yoke of bondage."

In the previous chapter (19) on Islam /Muslims, we discussed their origins in Ishmael and their establishment of social, religious, and judicial order through the works, of Mohammed, known as the Koran. Since Mohammed lived about six hundred years after Jesus, Muslims accept Jesus as a prophet. The journey of the Muslims, from Mohammed to the present, has been one of numerical growth. It has also been one of religious and political growth.

True Arabs are the descendants of Ishmael. They were the Nomadic people of Arabia. As I shared in the earlier chapter on Muslims, the Arabs were never an organized group. From AD 600 to recent years the organization of Muslims into the Islamic faith has grown. It has become the predominant religion of the Middle East and northern Africa. Many groups of people in many of the countries have adopted the faith of Arab Muslims.

The Muslim faith has a significant role to play in the last days. Their objective is to make the whole world a Muslim world under Sharia. There are two roadblocks in their way: the Jewish people and Christians. There are also two base things these two groups possess that make it impossible to conquer them: their faith and their military power.

Sharia and democracy cannot coexist. Muslims believe that Sharia treats everybody equal and therefore is democracy. Judeo-Christian based democracy practices treating everybody equal regardless of religion. In other words you can be a Muslim in a Christian country such as America and be treated equally in the court system. You cannot be a Christian in a Muslim-based country and be treated by any other way than through the Sharia law of the Muslim religion.

In 1928 Hason Al-Banna's founded the Muslim Brotherhood. It was established to be an outreach for the message of Islam through preaching, social outreach, and exemplary life. Its practice in Egypt has been to confront Zionism and spread social justice through Sharia law. It was outlawed in 1952.

Since that time their leaders have run for offices through other political groups, independent and currently have a strong voice in Egypt for the rebuilding of that country.

Over the centuries the Muslims have spread out across the world. They have concentrated on the Middle East and in the last three decades have focused heavily on western Europe. They have gone about methodically infiltrating America by planting their people in society and focusing on the political, judicial system.

It is clear that we are in the last days from the Muslim perspective. They have increased the pressure and their presence dramatically on many fronts. The militant wing of Islam is supported by the passive political / religious wing of Muslims.

The Arab Spring, which took place in sixteen Middle East countries in 2011 that appears as a cry for democracy by the masses, appears also to have a strong involvement by the Muslim Brotherhood.

In Egypt, the Christians who were protected under Mubarak are now being killed and their churches and homes destroyed. In Iraq the small Christian community that existed without great persecution now is fleeing for their lives out of the country.

The leaders of some Middle East countries have asked their Muslim followers to eradicate the Jews from the face of the earth. In New York City Muslims marched in what they called, the "Third Intifada," which called for complete Jewish genocide.

In Dearborn, Michigan, a Muslim festival is held on public property and streets in which Christians and non-Muslims could not attend by law. In civil courts in America, Muslims have asked to be tried with Sharia law, and it is being considered.

Psalms 83:2-7

"Thine enemies make a tumult: and they that hate thee have lifted up the head. They have taken crafty counsel against thy people, and consulted against thy hidden ones. They have said, come, let us cut them off from being a nation; that the name of Israel may be no more in remembrance. For they have consulted together with one consent: they are Confederate against thee: the Tabernacles of Edom and the Ishmaelites; of Moab and the Hagarenes; Gebal, Ammen, Amalek; the Philistines with the inhabitants of Tyre."

It appears to me that there is a pattern with the Muslims. They say that they come in peace and then they establish their culture among other cultures in cities and communities around the world. In these communities they seem to get along with other cultures, are peaceable and law abiding citizens. Little by little, their community grows in certain cells more strongly. For example, one Muslim man recently pleaded innocent to running over his daughter on purpose because he was justified based on his religious beliefs.

The next level we see is rallies and marches and intimidations about their desire to have their justice system in place. Look at France, Germany, and the United Kingdom and how the governments have to make laws to protect the citizens of their country from violence by these groups. A poll taken of students and faculty at a university in the United Kingdom, students reveals that 40 percent want Sharia law to rule.

One leader of a banned Islamist organization was quoted as saying that his ultimate objective was the domination of the world by Islam. In December of 2010 WikiLeaks shared a classified U.S. diplomatic cable soon after that the Obama administration directed its embassy employees in the United Kingdom to conduct outreaches to help empower the British-Muslim community.

Sharia is not democracy. Under Sharia women are second-class citizens, all women. They do not have a choice of being out of their house alone or to choose what garments they wear when they are out and about. In Egypt, 90 percent of the women have suffered female genital mutilation. Young girls have no clue about life due to the fact that at such a young age they can be given in marriage to a man of any legal age. According to Islam a man can be married for as little as one hour and then divorce. Limbs are severed for certain crimes. Non-Muslims are required to pay tax for not being Muslims. Christians cannot speak of their faith, or they can be imprisoned. If a Muslim converts to Christianity they can be put to death. To say a derogatory thing against Mohammed requires the death penalty in some countries. To disrespect the Koran, such as destroying it improperly, one may be given a lifetime sentence in prison.

These things are reprehensible to you and I who live in America and take it for granted as though it can't be lost.

The 9/11 events of airplanes being hijacked and flown into buildings are just one example of the militant wing of the Islamic movement. It is the belief of many Islamics, because it is written in the Koran, that to kill an infidel (that is any Christian or Jew or any one of another faith) is a glorious thing with great rewards.

In short, while we see Muslims who are peaceful we must understand that given time and enough liberty, their militancy will come out and they will fulfill their mission of Islam and Sharia for every person at any cost. The militant Islamics will press the more peaceful believers into violence.

One of the ways they can be successful in the United States is to develop their culture into a strong enough voting base to turn the laws of this country over to them. *America, Wake Up!* We have nothing in place in America that protects our Judeo-Christian based democracy from being overturned a piece at a time through judicial process. It is just a matter of time until our culture is a minority and other cultures will change our laws. There arc estimates today that France will be Islamic by 2050. If you are twenty years old now there is a great chance you will live to see this happen. France was a strong Christian nation and ally with similar beliefs in their freedom just fifty years ago. Now they are facing a potential country where they will not be able speak of the time there were Christians in the land.

In the last days the Muslim/Islamic people will be a strong and formidable force throughout the world. Their target is to make every country, every person a Muslim by persuasion with words or the sword; it matters not.

This is not to make you fear or hate Muslims or even radical jihadists, but rather to help you understand the biblical perspective of this particular group. I hope you don't stop reading here and throw the book across the room. When you get to the end of the book if you feel that I'm telling you things just to get you agitated; then throw the book across the room, out the door, into the fire or even mail it back to me with a nasty gram.

Please bear in mind the point of this book is that Jesus is returning because the bride is wonderfully ready, not because the world is so bad or the church is so persecuted.

CHAPTER 32

The Last Days:
The Jews—
A Special People

Deuteronomy 26:18-19

"And the Lord has avowed thee this day to be His peculiar people, as He hath promised thee, and that thou shouldest keep all his Commandments; and to make thee high above all nations that He has made, in praise, and in Name, and in honor; and that thee mayest be an holy people unto the Lord thy God, as he hath spoken."

The Jews are a special people to God because the Messiah was born through the lineage of Isaac. Abraham recognized that Isaac was the chosen son born by his wife, Sarah. Ishmael was the wild child more of the Egyptian woman Hagar. Through the lineage of Isaac and Jacob (Israel) came the family known as the Israeli's.

God gave Abraham the land that Israel inhabits today. Abraham gave the land to Isaac as a sign of God's blessing Isaac's family. Abraham gave Ishmael gifts but no land. Since that time there have been wars between the two families over that land, even to this day. When Joshua brought Israel back from Egypt they had to fight to repossess their land.

Years later they spent time in captivity by the Persians, Greeks, and Romans. Around AD 70 Romans decided to annihilate the Jews from the face of the earth. The final battle was at Masada. The Jews fled and the Arabs possessed the land. While the Jews lived in the promised land, it flourished and became very productive. When the Jews were driven out and other empires occupied the land, it became barren and not useful under the Muslim rule from AD 635 to AD 1917. The country became desolate and the "Palestinian" Muslims left en masse.

In the mid-1800s Jews fleeing persecution in Russia and Europe fled to the Palestine land. With some help from wealthy people, such as the Rothschild's, the Jews began purchasing land from the Muslim Ottoman Turks. The Jews then turned their homeland once again into a successful living area. The poor Muslims from surrounding country's came to work for the Jews. It is mostly these migrant workers descendants who call themselves the Palestinians today.

Prime Minister Netanyahu recently told American President Barack Obama that Israel could not return to the boundaries set by the 1967 war. He said that would breach the security of Israel and their country would fall to the military powers of the Muslims around them. He went on to state that the Jews would never again allow themselves to be taken out of their country and enslaved.

It is said that Israel has over two hundred nuclear devices and would destroy all the countries that attack them even if that meant their own destruction in so doing. This would be a last-ditch effort. They have simply made it clear for them to die in the heat of battle would be better than to be annihilated through surrender.

The Jewish people, adhering to the Mosaic Law and their Talmud have developed a democracy on which all democracies in the world are founded. They also have a relationship with God that gives them great faith that is based on God's peace and grace.

Since Abraham there has never been a stronger, more resolute, and more peaceful Israel. The mark of Israel in the last days squarely lies in this fact. I do not have any persuasion about the way Israel will be dealt with after Jesus comes to take his bride away. I firmly believe, however, that we are in the last days. Israel is going to face a showdown with the Muslim countries someday in the near future. The fact is that we face a gigantic and aggressive Muslim empire in the Middle East. With extreme Islam screaming for the eradication of Israel; and Israel declaring peace or Holocaust; every Christian should be alert to the fact that we are on the threshold of the end. Again I want to share with you that Jesus is not going to come back to earth and snatch the Bride away because things are so bad on this earth.

This is simply a wake-up call that we are in the last days.

The Jewish state of Israel is the strongest and most resolved democracy on earth today. Every American should understand now that if we weaken and do not stand the ground that Israel is we will fall. If we sell Israel down the river of tyranny and they fall, we will also fall. America needs to thank Israel for their stand and resolve to stand with them. They are blessed of God and know it and are acting responsibly to their faith. God will reward that. We (America) are falling into apathy, doubt, and delusion, and if unchanged will get the *change* that is promised and it will not include freedom or Jesus.

Let every person who loves Jesus or even believes in God stand up and vote at the polls only for the candidate that will stand with us to bring our country back to Christ. I am talking to you. It is time to stand up and be accountable to God alone and proclaim this country for Jesus.

How you say?

> *Live the life of a bride about to be married. Make your life all about the one you love, JESUS.*

CHAPTER 33

The Last Days: Christians— Becoming a Bride

Ephesians 4:11-16

"And God gave some, apostles; and some, prophets, and some, evangelist; and some pastors and teachers; for the perfecting of the saints, for the work of the ministry, for the edifying of the body of Christ: until we all come in the unity of the faith, and of the knowledge of the son of God, unto a perfect man, unto the measure of the stature of the fullness of Christ: that we henceforth be no more children, tossed to and fro, and carried about with every wind of doctrine, by the sleight of men, and cunning craftiness, whereby they lie in wait to deceive: but speaking the truth in love, may grow up into him and all things, which is the head, even Christ; from whom the whole body fitly joined together and compacted by that which every joint supplieth, according to the effectual working in the measure of every part, maketh increase of the body unto the edifying of itself in love."

Jesus is coming for his bride. I believe he's coming soon. I believe we're in the "last days" that Joel spoke of regarding the pouring out of that spirit. The true church is the bride of Christ.

> *Revelation 19:7-8*
>
> *"Let us be glad and rejoice, and give honor to him: for the marriage of the Lamb is come and his wife hath made herself ready. And to her was granted that she should be arrayed in fine linen, clean and white: for the fine linen is the righteousness of saints."*

As I have shared in previous chapters, I grew up in a home with parents who taught salvation through the blood of Jesus. From the time I was a small child I heard the words "Jesus is coming soon." With only one exception: all of the signs that caused people to believe Jesus is coming soon had to do with the evil increasing in the world and the Jews returning to their homeland. The one exception is the pouring out of the spirit as evidenced in the Pentecostal churches experiencing speaking in tongues, healings, and physical phenomena which caused them to believe.

What I have discovered, and share with you this book, is that the most compelling and complete prophetical relation of the coming of Jesus lies in the developments in the relationship of Jesus and his bride. It is what's happening in the church in the last days that causes me to believe he's coming soon.

When a man and a woman discover each other, and it occurs to them that they may want to pursue each other toward an end, possibly of marriage, they go through a number of steps. They are the basic get acquainted, learn about their superficial interest and behavior, spend time with each other and learn their basic values and belief systems, learn and understand deeper values and character traits, and finally, they feel they are in love.

When they discover that they love each other, they open the deeper parts of their heart and begin to melt their individual ideals into one ideal. In this phase, which usually occurs from the time of engagement until the time of marriage, they allow their emotions, convictions, and motivations to be challenged and refined by their new love.

It is in this last phase that the relationship goes from an intellectual understanding and knowledge of their loved one to a relationship of community participation in the guidance of their character. Their behavior becomes increasingly acceptable to each other. This is not because they have learned to act according to the other person's wishes, but their hearts are changed to be more like each other.

Ephesians 5:31, "For this cause shall a man leave his father and mother, and shall be joined unto his wife: and they two shall be one flesh."

The couple becomes married, they become one in all ways. In their hearts and in their character they have become one through the courtship before marriage. Many marriages fail today because they did not take the time to understand or choose to become one before they say "I do."

The "last days" are the days when Jesus and his bride (church) become one. Jesus prayed for this to his father right before he was crucified.

John 17:21-22, "That they all may be one; and thou, Father, art in me, and I in thee, that they also may be one

in us: that the world may believe that thou hast sent me.
And glory which thou gavest me I have given them; that
they may be one, even as we are one."

This is prophetical. Jesus prayed that this would happen in the future. Becoming one does not happen overnight. It takes time. Learning about Jesus, adjusting our character to fit with his, and making choices to move deeper into the relationship has taken centuries.

In the years from Christ's death until the death of the apostles there was a tremendous outpouring of God's Spirit. This was an emotional and life-changing time for the church. The freshness of the relationship with Jesus and the Holy Spirit made the church poignant and alive. Over the next one thousand five hundred years, the growth of the relationship was steady, with some very rocky road to traverse, with the church not displaying the character of Christ so much, but certainly their intent was to continue to grow the relationship as far as their revelation allowed.

From around 1500 until 1900, there was a proliferation of understanding the Bible and therefore God deepened the intellectual part of the relationship. This time period was all about learning the behaviors that are acceptable to God. The doctrines of salvation, water baptism, the virgin birth, vicarious sacrifice of Christ, resurrection and ascension being the basic focus. From these doctrines other beliefs grew through study and common practice.

In the early 1900s a new thing began to happen. There was a similar experience happening to Christians across America and around the world. This new thing was called Pentecost. I believe it was what Hosea referred to as the former and latter rain.

Hosea 3:4-5, "For the children of Israel shall abide many
days without a cane, and without the prints, and without

a sacrifice, without an image, and without an Ephod, and
without teraphim; afterward shall the children of Israel
return, and seek the Lord their God, and David their
king; and shall fear the Lord and His goodness in the
latter days."

Here Hosea speaks of Israel's return to her homeland after a long period of being without a country or a leader. He then says they will be a country for God and it will be established in the last days. This I believe occurred in 1948. This establishes a time when the pouring out of the former and latter rain should occur.

Hosea 6:3, "Then shall we know, if we follow on to know
the Lord: His going forth is prepared as the morning; and
He shall come unto us as the rain, as the latter and former
rain unto the earth."

In the days of early Pentecost from the early 1900s until the current time we have seen that former rain. It has been a repeat of the days of the apostles in AD first century.

A change is occurring in the way we relate to God. Instead of focusing on what Christians do the focus is shifting to what people are. This is the sign of the approaching winter rain. We are between spiritual pouring outs of rainstorms so to speak. The clouds of the Shekinah glory that poured the rain of the Holy Spirit anointing has somewhat abated in the last thirty years. However, the clouds are beginning to form of that latter rain. This latter rain is the final connecting of the hearts of the believers (the bride) and Jesus himself. This is the final part of courtship between Jesus and his bride before the wedding that takes place in heaven.

The key to the pouring out is in the church's understanding that we no longer can live independently of the Holy Spirit guiding us into that perfect relationship with Jesus and that we can no longer live an independent relationship with one another but that it must be just as intimate as it is with Jesus. We must become one with each other as we become one with Christ, just like Jesus prayed that we would be one as he and the father are one.

The true mark of the "last days" is the obvious display of what Paul shared in Ephesians 4. It is all about growing up into a collective body who has the same love, commitment, character, and full stature of Jesus. It is about becoming one in unity that is not shaken or swayed by the forces who are putting pressure on the bride to disbelieve in the last days.

I make a special note to the fifteenth verse where Paul says we establish this by speaking forth truth in love. This indicates that we must understand the truth that lies deep within us through Christ before we can speak truth.

The way that we have been trained in the last few centuries as Christians deals with our outward behavior. I grew up with an old saying that we live by the dos and don'ts of religion. Yet in my relationship with God I have found it is not so much about what I do or don't do as it is about what is deep inside of me and my character.

I have discovered that hidden, painful events from as early as our earliest childhood even into adulthood cause us to mask some of our character traits because of fear and shame. When we try to handle them in our own effort we cut off God from doing his work. When we call out to God, confess our pain, repent of our selfishness, and let him work his miracles in our heart: we begin to have that intimate relationship with him.

It is in this area that we see the entrance to the final steps of receiving the latter rain.

I heard throughout my childhood, through the Ministry training, and in sermons throughout my life that Jesus sets us free from sin. We used to sing a song titled *He Set Me Free*. I sang that song with all of my heart only to discover after many years that I really was not free. I found that I had things deep inside of me that I was not pleased with and it hindered me from an intimate relationship with God. It was not until I took an issue to the Lord and let him take control that I could be set free from anything.

Jesus said, "The Son therefore shall make you free, and He whom the Son sets free is free indeed." This does not just happen because we love Jesus and lay asking him to set us free. It happens when we face the truth about ourselves deep within those caverns of our character. When we take it to Jesus, face the truth, let him work his love in us, and allow our character to change and become a different person, is when we are set free.

This is a mark of the last days: when the bride is being set free of deep hidden pains. This is when we begin to see God bless in a very different way than ever before.

On the Isle of Patmos Jesus revealed himself to John and spoke of things to come. The first thing Jesus told John was that in the last days there would be seven different problems with the church. The first issue that he spoke of was to the church of Ephesus.

Revelation 2:4, "Nevertheless I have somewhat against thee, because thou hast left thy first love." When the apostles and others dispersed after the day of Pentecost they had that zeal and exuberance that can only be expressed from the first love. It was all about Jesus. They told everybody they could about their newfound relationship. They forsook everything else and followed the Holy Spirit's voice.

They were endowed with power not only to do miracles but to show forth that deep intimacy with Jesus after he had set them free. This beautiful display of first love affected those that saw it so dynamically that they gave their hearts to the Lord and followed Jesus.

The call then is for the church to come back to our first love and watch God work in our lives. The church is grown in a relationship with God, which has grown as well from the first church days. But as we approach the coming of Christ and our eternal marriage with him, they must find that there is joy and exuberance of our lives being all about him and the intimacy we get to share with him.

When we can get beyond our selfishness and make it all about Jesus, and let our lives begin to reflect our new relationship we will see a pouring out of his spirit upon us as it was prophesied in Hosea and Joel and as seen in the New Testament.

Do you believe you are living in the last days? Do you love Jesus as much as you say? Are you saying right now, "but how and what do I do?"

Turn to Ephesians 4 and underline what you are supposed to be.

Come into the unity of faith

Spend time with God until you really know Jesus intimately with all your being.

Become perfect, equal to the measure and stature of Christ.

Grow up and stop thinking and acting like a child

Stand in your faith and don't be led around into fads and deceitful thinking

Quit being naïve

Speak out the truth in love

Grow up in unto him in **all** things

Fit in with other believers

Fellowship a lot and contribute to the collective bride

Do what edifies the whole body

These are not just words. This is what the bride of Christ will look like when Jesus comes and is being changed into this NOW.

CHAPTER 34

The Last Days:
Ready for Jesus
to Come

1 Thessalonians 4:16-18

*"The Lord Himself shall descend from heaven with a
shout, with the voice of the Archangel, and with the
Trump of God: and the dead in Christ shall rise first:
then we which are alive and remain shall be caught
up together with them in the clouds, to meet the Lord
in the air: and so shall we ever be with the Lord."*

The Bible contains sixty-six books in two sections called the Old Testament and the New Testament. It is a common belief that the Bible is broken down into various types of writings such as historical, poetic, prophetic, the Gospels, epistles, etc. Some people say they are New Testament Christians and others say they are full gospel. Some focus on prophecies while others focus on history and still others focus on New Testament living issues.

I would like to point you to a little different way of looking at the Bible.

I view the Bible as a single message from God. It tells the story of the bride of Christ. Though many people were inspired to write I believe that the compilation of the various books in the Bible we know as the King James Version is the inspired message of the bride. It tells us of the life of the bride from the beginning as an infant and how she grew into the fullness, an equal to the son of God, Jesus.

Since this Bible has only been given fully to all people around the world in the last few hundred years, and with all of the evidence that at the same time as the Bible has been distributed, all of the advances in other areas have been at the same time. It seems only reasonable to conclude that this Bible has been recorded, written, and saved for us in the last days.

It seems obvious to me that the Bible therefore is a complete story from God that shows the history of where the bride comes from, how she looks today, and what we can anticipate in the last days and at Jesus coming.

In short the Bible was given to us for the last days and therefore we can look at the New Testament as prophetical. When Jesus says the Holy Spirit will guide you into all truth he is speaking for everybody that is alive from that moment on but specifically is trying to help paint the picture of what the bride will look like when he comes back to earth. It is the story of Father God, his son Jesus, and the love relationship between the son and his bride.

In Ephesians 4, we see the progression of growth within the bride.

> *Ephesians 4:10-16*
>
> *"He that descended is the same also that ascended up far above all heavens, that He might fill all things. And God gave some, apostles; and some, prophets; and some, evangelist; and some pastors and teachers; for the perfecting of the saints, for the work of the ministry, for the edifying of the body of Christ: **until** we all come in the unity of the faith, and of the knowledge of the son of God, unto a perfect man, unto the measure of the stature of the fullness of Christ: that we henceforth be no more children, tossed to and fro, and carried about with every wind of doctrine, by the sleight of men, and cunning craftiness, whereby they lie in wait to deceive: but speaking the truth in love, may grow up into Him and all things, which is the head, even Christ; from whom the whole body fitly joined together and compacted by that which every joint supplieth, according to the effectual working in the measure of every part, maketh increase of the body unto the edifying of itself in love.*

When Jesus left earth by ascension he left the work of preparing and organizing the church for his return in the hands of specific leaders. These leaders are apostles, evangelist, prophets, pastors, teachers, helpers, governors, deacons, and elders. Their work specifically was for the perfecting of the saints, the work of ministry and the building up of the body of Christ.

The church, since that day, has grown and flourished and become strong because of the leadership of these people following the plan of building up and perfecting the body of Christ.

Unfortunately, the church has become comfortable with its leadership having the burden of producing growth, while the members simply sit back and live their life in their comfort zones. They think, "As long as I do what I'm told to do, all will be well." Hence, they do not grow any further. Nothing could be farther from truth than that statement. God intends for all of us to grow fully into the image and likeness of Jesus the groom . . .

That first word in the thirteenth verse is *until*. This word is a transitional word that means that which preceded it will exist until that which follows takes place.

So God never intended for us to always have pastors doing the work of the ministry. His intention is for us to get the point of why ministry exists and to step into that maturity.

Next in the thirteenth verse God makes it very clear where we are supposed to be going. The work of this ministry is to bring us to the unity of our faith and have a complete knowledge of Jesus. We then become perfect in the measurement against Christ perfection. From this our character is the same in stature as the character of Christ.

When our character and stature is equal to that of Christ, then we move on to the fourteenth, fifteenth, and sixteenth verses. These verses show us how our behavior reflects our character. For instance, in the sixteenth verse he says the whole body should be fitly joined together. This means we work together in unison without fussing and feuding within the body.

Over the years I have pointed out to hundreds people, who I believe dearly love the Lord, that thirteen times in the New Testament alone God says for us to be perfect.

I have been amazed that absolutely every time people have said, "Nobody can be perfect."

I then asked the question, "Then why does the Bible say for us to be perfect?"

The best answer I ever get is "It just means complete."

Yet in Ephesians it says that the reason we have a pastor and evangelist is so that we will become perfect just like Jesus.

When confronted with this specific Scripture people fallback to the "I am not responsible for this; it means we will be made perfect when we go to heaven."

If that were so, you would say that as soon as you were just about perfect, God will sweep you off to heaven and then you are transformed and made perfect. Instead the picture is painted for us of how we will behave here on earth after we have become perfected.

As I shared in the last chapter, concerning the bride growing up in the last days to the full stature of Christ, there is growth. In the last days we develop that character perfection. It is through the pouring out of the Spirit and our willingness to face the truth that transforms us into one with Christ.

So what are the attributes of the character of Jesus?

Perfect, full of knowledge, one with the father, submitted, humble, reconciling, loving, full of faith, does not seek his own, long-suffering; possesses love, joy, peace, gentleness, goodness, seeks his father's will, loves, and practices truth,

What will the church look like when Jesus comes?

All of the people who are part of the live bride when Jesus comes will be mature, able to see through false teachings, speak the whole truth, have grown up in Christ in every way, get along in pure harmony with everyone else in the body, and the church will be in a growth phase adding many people to the body.

There will be no need for preachers to tell us how to live. We will be totally dependent collectively and individually on the Holy Spirit's teaching and guidance.

> *John 14:26, "But the Comforter which is the Holy Ghost, whom the Father will send in my name, He shall teach you all things, and bring all things to your remembrance, whatsoever I have said unto you."*

> *John 16:13, "When He, the Spirit of truth, is come, He will guide you into all truth: for He shall not speak of himself; but whatsoever He shall hear, that shall He speak: and He will show you things to come."*

God gave us pastors and others mentioned earlier to guide us into the maturity of Jesus. It was never intended by God that we should have pastors and teachers telling us how to live right up to the rapture. Perhaps it has not even entered the minds of the Bride of Christ, let alone its leadership, that there could be a different way. Just as children grow up, mature, and begin to determine life for themselves as opposed to having their parents tell them what to do and how to behave, how to think; so the church must grow up, becoming mature, and to rely upon the Holy Spirit to make them one and prepare them for their coming king.

The perfection of Jesus that is to be displayed in the church is the same sense of the oneness between each member of the church as there is between God and the church. When we reach that perfection we will no longer need the parent (preachers, etc.) telling us how to live but will rely on the Holy Spirit.

We then become dependent on our personal relationship with the Holy Spirit to guide us into the oneness and fullness of Jesus as described in Ephesians.

Can you now begin to see that complete growth from birth to maturity of the bride and the matrimony of Jesus to the bride is not only spoken of in the Bible but is the story of the Bible?

In the end, the book of Revelation declares, "I will be their God and they will be my people." This is what it is all about. The Bible is the story of how God accomplishes this. He uses the illustration of his son and the bride of his son, to help us understand, with our human flawed mind, that he will have a body of people who love him with all of the capacity that he loves them. God created man with the power to choose, that man would choose to love God, so that God would have eternally guaranteed love by man. This is the story of how that occurs. When we as a people grow up into the marvelous mature person as Jesus, God will say it is time and send his son to take us home and forever we shall be his people.

CHAPTER 35

The Last Days: How Then Shall We Live?

Acts 1:8

"But ye shall receive power, after that the Holy Ghost is come upon you: and ye shall be witnesses unto me both in Jerusalem, and in all Judea, and in Samaria, and unto the most part of the Earth."

By now we should all be convinced we live in the "last days." Based on what I have shared with you in previous chapters I would like now to look at what is ahead for this world and the bride of Christ who lives in it.

"There Is No God"

That group which we call the "there is no God" have an agenda as do all the groups. This group seeks to destroy Christians and put off acknowledgment of God out of their presence. The absolute rejection of God, his Son, and his people leaves them hopeless with the spiritual void in their lives filled with hatred toward those who are filled with the goodness of God.

There are those godless people who do not care if we exist as long as we exist somewhere besides around them. Some of this group such as countries like China, North Korea, and much of Russia are more militant.

Be assured this group seeks to destroy Christians. Their focus is to tear down the democracies of America, Canada, Australia, United Kingdom, and western Europe. The reason these democracies exist is because Christians developed a democracy centuries ago. The war they make is targeted at Christians.

"The Designer God"

This group, consisting of many groups of people, each person has their god. They are given to the god they have created for themselves. They do not want the light of God shed on their sins because they have chosen to go their way and live in darkness.

They reject Christians because they are the children of light. They will fight for the legal supremacy in democracies to make laws that require Christians to restrict their voice to silence and then acknowledge, and even celebrate, their ungodly beliefs and practices.

In the past chapters regarding these people we talked about specific groups, their agenda and the determination with which they pursue the accomplishment of their agenda.

The Muslim/Islamists

This group seeks the outright annihilation of all Christians and Jews. Their agenda is to make all people, by any means necessary including force and murder, to become Islamists.

While their target seems to be America and Israel, the more realistic target is democracies: but their goal is removing Christians and instilling Sharia law around the world.

Their threat to Christians is through the cunning method of coexistence until their culture dominates the Christian culture and then they take over the Christians' country. Look carefully at the lifestyles of Muslims, Christians, and Jews who live in Sharia-governed countries.

The Jews

The Jews, whether they live in Israel or elsewhere around the world, are our best friends. God has put his hand upon them because he has a special place for them not only in the total history of this earth but in heaven to come.

While America is the most powerful nation on earth, Israel is the most powerful nation in the Middle East. We stand together or we will fall from being divided.

The Christians

Jews and Christians are allies. As the end approaches in these last days, we have a few things deeply in common. We both have Messiah coming for us, a deep desire to love and bless others, the path of peace in our hearts, and the same God of love and compassion that we worship.

But we are at war with the other three groups. It is not that we have declared war, nor do we hate them; but that war has been declared by them upon us. Through democracy we declared that we could each worship God as we believed. Our country of America was founded upon Christian principles and a strong belief, not only by our founding fathers but also by those voting constituents who placed them in power, that our faith in God is what makes our country strong.

The war being waged against us is the war of Satan against God. He wages his war through his minions against the children of God. We must continuously remind ourselves that we are not the aggressors. That is because these groups see us as accusers because our faith and morals cause them to feel guilty before God. In turn they accuse us of attacking them. Yet it is they who seek to destroy just as Satan seeks to destroy. For them there is no peaceful coexistence. They will never experience peace as long as we exist to shine the light of Jesus on their dark souls.

How then shall we live? Shall we bow to Baal and Ashtoreth? Shall we strike back with force?

If you've read the book of Revelation and other excerpts from other books in the Bible, you know that the end is where God destroys the wicked and we the bride live with him forever. It is the time between now and then that we are concerned with.

We as Christians must recognize that our adversary is Satan and that Satan works through those people who serve him.

So to those who wish to destroy us by destroying our culture and then take away our freedom and democracy through political, judicial, and parliamentary methods, we can respond by protecting our culture, constitution, and parliamentary systems by enacting laws that protect us.

To those who wish to destroy us by enacting laws requiring us to embrace those behaviors that are offensive, we can vote in lawmakers, through the Christian vote, who will stand for the values that we as Christians believe in and our country was founded upon.

To those who wish to take our country by force through terrorism and military action, we can stand strong and defend democracy.

Will we defend and stand for what we believe in? If we do, it may delay the inevitable global war. The evil forces of this world are going to continue their evil ways and grow in strength. All of these groups who oppose the Lord will someday unite and be strong enough to wage that battle against God and the countries that stand for him.

How Then Shall We Live?

John 14:26, "But He, which is the Holy Ghost, whom the Father will send in my name, He shall teach you all things, and bring things to your remembrance, whatsoever I have said unto you"

John 16:13, "When He, the Spirit of truth, is come, He will guide you into all truth: for He shall not speak of Himself; but whatsoever He shall hear, that shall He speak: and He will show you things to come."

As I shared in other chapters Jesus is not coming back to fix or set right this looming and threatening situation. He is coming back for his bride. He is coming for a bride who is his equal. He is coming for a bride who yearns for him. He is coming for a bride who is totally in love and consumed with his presence and his love for her.

He is coming for a bride in purity and white garments without spot or blemish (Ephesians 5:27), perfect, holy, humble, and eternally committed to the worship and lifting up of God.

He is coming for a bride who takes pleasure not in her own will but in his will. He is coming for a bride who is only concerned about his pleasure. He is coming for a bride who seeks truth, no matter how painful, and rises up and walks in truth and light before all others.

We *then must live* together on this earth as one with God and each other. We must fall upon our knees, humble ourselves, repent of our selfishness, and let the Holy Spirit fill us with the love of Jesus. We must look deep within our own lives and let the Holy Spirit reveal and remove those things that we hold for ourselves and those deep hurts that create pain when we start to deal with them.

We must rise up filled with the spirit and bond with our fellow Christians who are doing the same. Take off these tarnished robes of self-indulgence, fraternization with allowances and tolerances that come from the world, and put vile stains upon our garments. We must put on our white robes of right standing, write the name of Jesus upon them, and walk in the ways of righteousness and holiness, separated unto the Lord.

Having rid ourselves as a body of Christ of the diseases of the spiritual, emotional, intellectual, and physical immorality and ungodliness, making ourselves wholly dependent upon the Holy Spirit to keep us, guide us, and prepare us for our savior who was and is and is to come.

We must lay aside every whim of doctrine that separates us as a church, from the church, and person from person. We must cling to one another who are washed white as snow and build that strong bond of a single united body across America to every democracy and to every person who sees Jesus in us and wants to follow him.

There is no other way. There is no hope in any way but through Jesus. As much as Jesus laid down his life for us, so he requires us to lay down our life for him.

While we must fight for the survival of our country and our freedom and our way of life, it is futile to believe that we will ultimately win this war on this earth. We will not. That is not our purpose, our goal, or God's plan.

Our objective on this earth is very simple. We are to prepare for the coming of Jesus and to keep all those God gives us.

> *Matthew 28:18-20*
> *"And Jesus came and spoke unto them saying, all power is given unto me in heaven and in earth. Go ye therefore and teach all nations, baptizing them in the name of the Father, and of the Son, and of the Holy Ghost: teaching them to observe all things whatsoever I have commanded*

you: and lo I am with you always, even unto the end of the world."

Mark 16:15-18
"And he said unto them, go ye into all the world, and preach the gospel to every creature. He that believes and is baptized shall be saved: but he that believes not shall be damned. And these signs shall follow them that believe; in my name shall they cast out devils: they shall speak with new tongues; they shall take up serpents; and if they drink any deadly thing, shall not hurt them; they shall lay hands on the sick, and they shall recover."

Acts 1:8
"You shall receive power, after that the Holy Ghost is come upon you: and ye shall be witnesses unto me both in Jerusalem, and in all Judea, and in Samaria, and unto the outermost part of the Earth."

When we empty ourselves of our selfishness and let the Holy Spirit transform us into the image that he wants, we will then be ready to teach the world the true transformation power of Jesus's name.

There is not anything we can say or anything we can do that will change another human being. It is the power of the Holy Spirit convicting us, our submission to the cleansing work of Jesus in our heart, and the willingness to let him rule our lives that convicts others. That power and purity is what the world fights against. It is what we Christians have fought against and understand that we need to surrender to our Lord.

We have tasted the former rain in the 1900s. It has been a pause in the mighty outpouring of the Holy Spirit transforming lives and setting captives free. The coming of the evil pressure that seeks to destroy us also comes as a cloud on the horizon that is going to shower our spiritual lives with the power and blessing and demonstration of the Holy Spirit.

That latter rain is beginning to sprinkle. The clouds of the Shekinah glory are starting to form. Jesus is coming. Set not your sights on the enemy's position. Be not dismayed or fearful. But look only to the coming savior, groom, and king.

Look to Jesus the author and finisher of your faith. Prepare for his coming. *Jesus is coming soon.*

John 17:21 That they may be one: as thou, Father, art in me, and I in thee, that they may be one in us: that the world may believe that thou hast sent me.

CPSIA information can be obtained at www.ICGtesting.com
Printed in the USA
LVOW060320190312

3654LV00004B/2/P